Th

LAKES

40 SHORTER WALKS

from **the EASY** *to*

the **ADVENTUROUS**

The author and publisher have made every effort to ensure that the information in this publication is accurate, and accept no responsibility whatsoever for any loss, injury or inconvenience experienced by any person or persons whilst using this book.

For Arlo

published by
pocket mountains ltd
The Old Church, Annanside, Moffat EH51 9HB
pocketmountains.com

ISBN: 978-1-9070250-2-0

Text copyright © Dominic North

Photography copyright © Dominic North

The right of Dominic North to be identified as the Author of this work has been asserted by him in accordance with the Copyright, Designs and Patents Act 1988

A catalogue record for this book is available from the British Library

All route maps are based on 1945 Popular Edition Ordnance Survey material and revised from field surveys by the author. © Pocket Mountains Ltd.

Printed in Poland

Introduction

The Lake District is England's pre-eminent National Park. Nowhere else is the pattern of mountain, wood and water so compactly and harmoniously arranged. Nowhere else is so artfully entwined within a network of paths, and nowhere else so draped in raw beauty. As a place to explore on foot, it is unique.

Contained within this guide are 40 walks travelling through the remarkable history and landscape of the Northern Lakes, from the environs of Shap in the east to the tip of Ennerdale Water in the west. Along the way find the diverse moods around Haweswater, Ullswater, Thirlmere, Keswick, Borrowdale, Newlands, Buttermere and the Western Lakes.

This is legendary walking country, and plenty of people have been this way before – and plenty more will come after – so what follows is an attempt to do something different, making the argument for new looks at old friends, for classics twisted, for overlooked corners and for places you have never been to, nor probably heard of. The sublime glories of the Lake District await – let this book be your companion.

About this guide

This is the first of two books spanning the National Park (a sister Southern Lakes volume follows). Here, the northern half is split into four areas: Ullswater, Haweswater and the eastern fringe; Thirlmere, Keswick and the northern hills; Derwentwater, Borrowdale & the central fells; Newlands, Buttermere & the western waters. There are only a few hard and fast means of splitting the area down, so to an extent there is an arbitrary element to these divisions, bound to provoke incredulity in some – 'how can you separate Keswick from Derwentwater?' You cannot, of course, so there is an inevitable crossover at the edges of the chapters. But the divisions do, I think, indicate general shifts in character from chapter to chapter. So, for instance, the Thirlmere, Keswick & the northern hills section represents – with a few glaring exceptions – perhaps the most overlooked terrain in the Northern Lakes. While the chapter on Derwentwater, Borrowdale & the central fells possesses the most concentrated scenery, it is also the busiest sliver of the north, its honeypot. Then, within the final western chapter, you find the purest remains of the old-time sleepy Lakes and the least outward sign of the explosion in visitor numbers.

The ground covered rises from easy valley strolls to adventurous mountain scrambles, but none are longer than, at most, a half-day of walking. This seemed crucial; for an area so compact, the emphasis is too often on the long days striving to the very highest mountains, or on looping ridges together into extended horseshoes. These are wonderful activities, but they rather overlook the snappy immediacy of much of the Northern Lakes' delights. There are forests to enjoy, ruins, mountain tarns, low and mid-height fells, waterfalls, lake shores, tranquil valleys, former quarries and mines, and, in the middle, a rugged town. These are all here, within digestible walks that – to extend the metaphor – are more convivial lunches than lengthy feasts. But the 'shorter' in the title does not always mean short (there are serious outings to St Sunday Crag, Great End and Blencathra here) – so take it as the relative term it is.

Each route sets out at its beginning the distance and height gained, the relevant Ordnance Survey (OS) 1:25,000 map (which should always be carried) and an indication of the walking time it will take. Duration will always be a moot point, with plenty of variables in play: fit, experienced walkers in spring sunshine will cover the same ground much quicker than novices in mist and rain. So, take it as a rough guide intended to assist with planning your day, and remember it does not allow for any of the stops that you may have in mind. The route map is also a general guide and is emphatically not intended for navigation.

Finally, the contents are arranged east to west, which (though sounding odd) is a general reflection of most people's experience when visiting the National

Park – they arrive from the east. So think of this as a journey into the Lakes, reaching its conclusion upon the desolate windswept top of Grike, about as far from the crowds as it is possible to get.

Getting around

Excepting Ullswater, Haweswater and the eastern fringe, which gravitate to the major regional centre of Penrith, Keswick is the hub around which the Northern Lakes spin: almost every transport link in the arc from the north to the northwest passes through, begins or terminates in Keswick. With major tourism and walking industries to serve, the public transport provision is pretty good too, particularly in the spring and summer when a number of additional bus services operate. These really are to be recommended, not least for environmental reasons, but also for relieving the frustration built by congested lanes and full car parks. What we all need, as Withnail puts it in *Withnail and I*, is 'harmony, fresh air and stuff like that'.

The most useful bus route is the year-round 78 (Borrowdale Rambler), running the length of Borrowdale from Keswick to Seatoller. This is an excellent means of reaching the Borrowdale start points in the third chapter; indeed, one route (p56) calls upon it for a return to Keswick. On a fine summer day, when an open-topped double-decker plies the route, the swaying journey above the wooded east shore of Derwentwater is worth it for its own sake.

The scenic and seasonal 77/77A (Honister Rambler) makes a rickety crossing of the Honister Pass en route to Buttermere and Crummock, calling also at Braithwaite and nipping at the edge of the Newlands Valley. The 208 (Ullswater Rambler), the 73/73A (Caldbeck Rambler) and the 74 (Osprey Bus) also have their valuable moments. See individual walks for which buses are recommended where.

Certainly the most memorable and evocative way of travelling is across the waters of one of the lakes – in the north that means the cheerful Keswick Launch on Derwentwater, and the famed 'steamers' (though long since diesels) criss-crossing Ullswater. Both should definitely be experienced (see the walks on p18 and p58); they operate year round, with extra sailings in the spring and, in particular, summer.

Despite all of the above, getting to some of the wilder places in the Northern Lakes can still be challenging without a car, especially in winter. While I encourage the use of public transport where feasible (www.traveline.info for more information), it has to be recognised that some of the best walking falls outside the reach of its providers' routes. So, I have not slavishly allowed public transport links to dictate the start/finish points of the routes chosen.

If cars are useful they can also be a problem, as evidenced by the erection of a lengthy sequence of hideous yellow signs

Sunset over the summit of Gowbarrow Fell, Ullswater ▶

deterring parking near the foot of Catbells. The answer when shackled to a car is to please exercise caution and consideration: ideally use a recognised car park (the start point will often steer you in that direction anyway); if this is not an option, a small, defined parking area should be. In the rare cases where it is not, be wary of blocking gateways, lanes and passing places. If in doubt, don't – you never know when a much larger vehicle (like a fire engine, say) may have to try and pass your inappropriately parked car.

Respecting the environment

The landscape of the Northern Lakes is remarkably resilient. Even so, millions of footsteps each year and robust weather systems combine to pose a considerable challenge – you don't have to look far to see evidence of severely eroded paths. A magnificent volunteer organisation called Fix the Fells (www.fixthefells.co.uk) is fighting back – they have repaired more than 100 of the worst paths, with over 70 more in their sights. Please play your part in the process, too: where a footpath exists, stick to it, rather than its fringe, walking single file if necessary. Try not to dislodge stones, build new cairns or cut across zigzags.

More generally, remember the farmers. Use stiles and gates where they exist and avoid leaving litter at all costs. Get to grips with the Countryside and Moorland Visitor's Codes. Keep dogs under control, ideally on a lead, especially when close to livestock and farms. Never come between a cow and her calf (with or without a dog). During lambing time, farmers are particularly and understandably sensitive. Remember this is a working landscape – a little respect goes a long way. All this helps to sustain a harmonious relationship between visitors and locals.

Safety

Do not underestimate the mountains, even if your trip into them is brief, and never underestimate how much more hostile the tops can be than the valleys, even in summer. Sudden weather changes, mist, cold, rain and snow are all part of walking in the Lakes, and while there is certainly a peculiar magic to remote fells in inclement weather, it is a situation best avoided unless properly equipped. So you will need to possess a map and compass and have the wherewithal to use them in less than ideal circumstances. Decent hillwalking boots are essential, as too are waterproofs, warm clothing, food and water. Know your own limitations and be sure to carry the relevant OS 1:25,000 map.

A mobile phone is a good idea, but not a panacea in the ills of an emergency – you might not get reception. Always carry a torch, first-aid kit, whistle and watch. Check the weather forecast before you leave and ensure someone knows where you are going and when you are due to return. Remember that in the end most Mountain Rescue calls come down to disorientation, slips and exhaustion.

If all this implies that walking in the Northern Lakes is an ordeal to be endured, be assured it is not. If you have the confidence of sound preparation, knowledge and equipment, you can ensure that your happy expedition remains just that, even when the weather turns, which at some point it will.

Access

The legal 'right to roam', applied locally in May 2005 under the Countryside and Rights of Way Act (2000), opened up new routes to walkers that may have previously been closed off, adding to existing rights of access in the Lake District. Indeed, that right is exercised to a lesser or greater extent in a number of the walks found in this book.

Under the Act, the public has new rights of access on foot to areas classified as open country (mountain, moor, heath and down) and registered commonland for recreational use. The right does not extend to activities such as cycling, canoeing, horse-riding or camping, though existing rights may already be in place for these activities on some land.

There are other restrictions in the Act: for instance, walkers must not damage any wall, fence, hedge, stile or gate in exercising their right of access, certain types of land are exempt and landowners have the right to limit access temporarily.

It is worth familiarising yourself with the legislation and what it means for walking in the area. The Ramblers' Association can provide more details through their website (www.ramblers.org.uk).

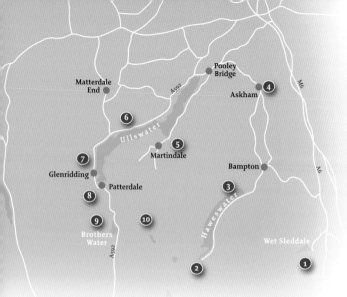

Like nowhere else in the Lake District, water defines the northeast. This is a landscape shaped by water, arranged around water and dictated to by the need for water, from the vast serpentine grandeur of Ullswater to the reservoirs of Haweswater and Wet Sleddale, lonely bodies harnessed by brooding dams. Water extravagantly decorates this landscape, from the languid curves of the River Lowther and the white falls of Aira Force to the pools and torrents of Measand Beck. Water clings stubbornly to the hills in rock-bound high tarns: Angle Tarn, a jumble of inlets and islets by the twin summits of Angletarn Pikes; Small Water, perhaps the prettiest of them all, tucked beneath the fierce crags of Harter Fell. And never far away, the stories of man's interaction with water, from the happy (the unlikely survival of Ullswater's graceful steamers), to the bittersweet (Donald Campbell's water speed record) and the sad (the flooding of Mardale).

Some valleys do not belong to water, but they are often the splintered ends and spurs. Two, squeezing between the mountains above the head of Ullswater, are Grisedale (for excursions low) and Deepdale, the door through to St Sunday Crag's wonderful east ridge (for expeditions high). Finally, discover the current of eccentricity flowing through the eastern fringe, from spendthrift aristocrats to a place in cult film history. Come to think of it, the northeast might be all the Lakes you need.

Wood Howe islet, Haweswater ▶

ULLSWATER, HAWESWATER AND THE EASTERN FRINGE

On the Withnail trail

Distance 7km Time 2 hours
Height gain 180m Map OS Explorer OL5
**Access Shap (some 3km from the closest
point on the walk, the weather station) is
linked to Kendal and Penrith by the 106
bus service**

**Wet Sleddale, an unassuming valley
close to Shap, was a key (and unlikely)
location for the revered cult film classic
Withnail & I. Follow the titular characters
to Sleddale Hall – aka Uncle Monty's
'Crow Crag' – on a brief but fascinating
walk from reservoir edge to moor edge.**

Start from the parking area at the
southern tip of Wet Sleddale Dam
(GR554114). Walk west along the track,
undulating above the southern shore of
the reservoir. After almost 1km, just
before the path passes through a
collapsing wall, take the gateway to the
left into the field above. Continue west,
crest to a wet depression (picking up
white-tipped waymarks) and then
descend through the next field over

coarse, reedy grass to the packhorse
bridge over Sleddale Beck: this is where
Withnail 'fished' with a shotgun (many of
the exterior shots were filmed by
Haweswater, though).

Walk up the far side, to a stile and a
wide stone path beyond, slanting right
into trees. Reaching a barn, cut up the
hummocky slope to Sleddale Hall, or
'Crow Crag' if you prefer (GR540113).
The derelict building, a shadow of its
celluloid glory, was sold in March 2009
with plans for renovation, so events may
have moved on. If possible, take a peek
into the farmyard and see if the graffiti
(almost all quotes from the film – it is
very quotable) still decorate the doors.

Return west to the track and continue
uphill, rounding a zigzag to meet a high,
contouring path (1h). Bear northeast to
the gate at the end of the field and out
onto the open moor. Taking the wall to
the right as a guide (a faint route runs

parallel roughly 50m from it, largely the work of quad bikes), follow the edge of the moor over an initial rise and then on a gradual descent across Stackhouse Brow.

Note the small conifer wood ahead to the right in the near distance – just past this go through an unmarked gate to the right. Trend right to pass the eastern tip of the conifers, descending further on a trenched track to just before a barn. Take the first gate on the left and walk towards the first in a band of solitary trees by the lower wall. Shadow the wall to a stile in the bottom corner and then cross the next field to a gate at the far end, just left of a barn. Go through this and a second gate 20m on to the left, and then drop down to the farm lane.

Turn left and follow the lane for 500m to a handsome, relatively new footbridge back over the beck. Walk up to the road, turning right along it to return to the car park. Pass the Met Office weather station, contemplate the dam and consider the kudos to be gained the next time the film arises in conversation (2h).

On holiday by mistake

Funny, intelligent and subversive, with a vivid undertow of farce, Withnail & I is settling with assurance into the canon of cinema's finest comedies. 'Withnail' (Richard E Grant) and 'I' (Paul McGann) are two dissolute actors fleeing late '60s London for the tranquility of a holiday in the country. They end up at 'Crow Crag', a freezing, shabby-chic Lake District cottage belonging to Withnail's lascivious Uncle Monty. The Wet Sleddale sequences are pivotal and an ever-growing attention has fallen upon the ruinous plight of the hall. After 20 years of allowing the house to slowly crumble, United Utilities shored up the structure and sold it at auction in March 2009. Planners permitting, buyer Sebastian Hindley intends a blend of tearoom and holiday accommodation for the building, to be accessible only by foot.

◀ The new bridge at Cooper's Green, Wet Sleddale

Haweswater skyline

▲ Harter Fell (778m)

Distance 7km **Time** 3 hours
Height gain 540m **Map** OS Explorer OL5
Access the nearest bus stop is at
Burnbanks for the infrequent 111/111A,
all the way at the other end of the lake

The 7km drive along the length of
Haweswater leads only to the eerie calm
of Mardale Head, a place with nothing to
indicate its presence other than a name.
Nowhere in the east is as lonely as here.
If that is not reason in itself to come
then consider the surrounding semicircle
of mountains, in particular the
wonderful Harter Fell, a traverse of
which reveals in miniature the full
ragged glory of the Lakes.

Start at the car park, Mardale Head
(GR469107). Walk through the fell gate at
the road end and take the well-made
bridleway curving left beneath trees to
Gatescarth Beck. Ascend by the beck

through a succession of small zigzags into
a combe (with the forbidding Harter Crag
to the right), moving from right of the
water to left as the beck splits into
tributaries. Rise to an open shoulder at the
head of the pass and bear west (before the
gate in the fence ahead) on an improved
path up the grassy eastern flank of Little
Harter Fell.

Gain the rocky head of the subsidiary
top, joining to the left a fence looping
across the fell to the summit. Cross
northwest over a saddle and then rise
steadily to the so-called 'third cairn' at
the end of Harter's northeast ridge, with a
striking view down the reservoir (1h30).
Bend sharply southwest with the fence
and cross the almost flat top of the ridge
for 600m to the summit (GR460093).
Along the way, you pass the first of a pair
of remarkable cairns – the second marks
the summit – its top fashioned from
former iron fenceposts twisted into metal

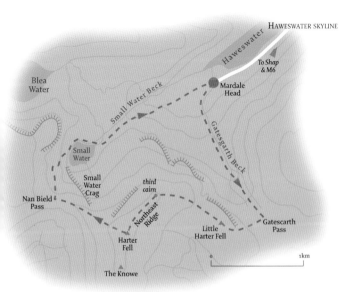

knots and flailing prongs, a particularly arresting sight emerging through mist.

From the summit, bear west to two prominent cairns, then down a narrow, steepening ridge, following a twisty but clear route over rocky terrain to the impressively solid shelter at the top of Nan Bield Pass (GR452096). Descend north through magnificent rock scenery to the teardrop-shaped Small Water, one of the

Lakes' finest mountain tarns. Skirt the western shore, cross the stepping stones at the outflow and drop down to the right of cascading Small Water Beck. Cross a tributary stream and bend right (northeast) around the slope to a kissing gate in the wall ahead. With an easing gradient, continue down in the same direction to a solid path, returning to the gate left at the start (3h).

The rising waters

With the completion of Haweswater Dam in 1935, the flooding of Mardale began. The water would eventually rise 29m above the natural lakes of the valley, High Water and Low Water, subsuming the already-demolished village of Mardale Green, The Dun Bull Inn, the Church of the Holy Trinity and many scattered farmsteads. (From time-to-time – notably in 1976, 1984 and 1995 – drought exposes the remaining walls.) This is the milieu that Cumbrian writer Sarah Hall drew upon for her first novel, Haweswater, published in 2002 and winner of the Commonwealth Writers' Prize, a story of a sheltered community and its impending doom.

◂ Looking down Haweswater to the semicircle of mountains above Mardale Head

Four Stones Hill

▲ Four Stones Hill (415m)

Distance 7km **Time** 2 hours 15
Height gain 250m **Map** OS Explorer OL5
Access Burnbanks is connected to
Penrith by the infrequent 111/111A
bus service

History endures in Mardale, from the
relics of Bronze Age settlement on Four
Stones Hill to the walls of the villages
flooded beneath Haweswater. This
charming walk of hummocky, rust-
coloured fells, waterfalls and watery
views casts the compelling, if rather
sad spell of a neglected corner of the
National Park.

Start at the turning to Burnbanks off
the Bampton-Haweswater road
(GR510162). Walk down the road towards
the hamlet, taking the gate to the right
after 150m (well before the houses). Rise

by a green path to the left of a wall.
As the wall bends right, continue directly
up the slope for a further 150m and
then turn left onto a path undulating
west through bracken. Pass beneath
sporadic crags onto a wide terrace with a
wonderful view down the length of
Mardale, and to the semicircle of
mountains at its head.

As the path turns north into a wide
trough, bear northwest along a sheeprun
to the top of the first of a trio of tightly
grouped knolls, Little Birkhouse Hill
(45 mins). Cross the hollow south to the
top of the second, the lower and
apparently no more significant Great
Birkhouse Hill (though seen from the
valley this appears the most imposing of
the three). A short hop west over a further
depression leads to the summit of the
third and highest, Four Stones Hill,

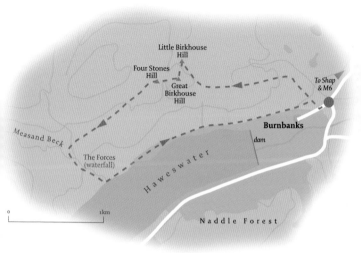

completing a short but entertaining ascent (GR491162). A dewpond (with what looks like a perimeter 'wall') and well-preserved hut circle are located just to the north (next to the path you eventually take), while the two stones (one standing, one leaning) are found southwest of these, though there was once presumably four. Linger here and contemplate the serenity, for the arrangement of construction, land and setting suggests a one-time significance, the source of which remains unknown.

Walk west on the path, which despite some reedy sections is surprisingly firm. Cross the footbridge over Measand Beck (GR482156) – note Fordingdale Bottom, a

superb hanging valley upstream – and follow the path descending by the western bank of The Forces, a collection of waterfalls, pools and cascades repaying the urge for a closer look.

Reaching the stony path just above the lake shore (1h30), re-cross the beck and head east back towards Burnbanks, a model settlement built for the dam workers. Rooted close to the water for the first 1km, the path then rises behind the wooded shield obscuring the dam. Rather than descending with the path through the trees into the hamlet, remain above the houses on a green path leading back to the gate you went through at the beginning of the walk (2h15).

The Lowther legacy

**Distance 10.5km Time 2 hours 30
Height gain 160m Map OS Explorer OL5
Access Askham is infrequently served by
the 111/111A bus service from Penrith**

**Nineteenth-century Westmorland and
Cumberland was the domain of the
grandee Lowthers, and Lowther Castle –
a vast neo-gothic palace east of Askham –
was the definitive statement of their
wealth. Long since a ruin, it forms the
centrepiece of this genial tour through
low farming country and the studied
beauty of ornamental parkland.**

Start at the community centre in the
centre of Askham (GR513236). Walk left
from the car park entrance, then left again
by Askham Stores down the road splitting
the broad banks of the village green. Bear
left after 300m (just before the last row of
whitewashed cottages on that side) to a
walled and impressively gated lane running
to the left of the grounds of Askham Hall,
the current Lowther seat. Pass between
farm buildings to a hedged track through

open country. Some 250m on, cross a stile
hidden in the field corner to the right,
making for a gate (green with a white top
bar, a Lowther Estate motif) opening to
woods in the opposite corner.

Join a wide, muddy path undulating
within the edge of the trees, passing right
of a small conifer plantation and on to a
narrow path winding on an elevated line
high above the River Lowther. Descend to
an estate road, turn right, cross the
elegant humpback Low Gardens Bridge
and walk up the now metalled road with
the castle ahead in the distance. Turn left
at the public road, rise for 350m to just
beyond a cattle grid and then turn right
on the road to Lowther (the village).

After 300m, cross a ladder stile flanked
by redundant pillars and, with an opening
vista to the ruin, descend through
parkland to the castle perimeter wall,
shadowing it past the gated archway and
around into woods (GR521239) (1h). Bear
left, forking right after 50m onto a
downhill track leading south out of the

◄ Lowther Castle: a shadow of its former glory

trees (note high to the left the fine
limestone escarpment, beyond which
is the soon-to-be-restored garden).

Follow the track past a ribbon
of conifers to reach the riverside.
Fork left to a fenced lane then,
100m short of the hamlet of Whale,
branch right into fields to skirt
beneath the farm buildings.
Emerging at a minor road turn
downhill to a T-junction and cross to
the bridleway opposite. Accompany
Whale Beck down to the river where a
bridge (GR517214) leads across to the
far bank. Turn downstream, cross a
tributary by a narrow footbridge and
keep right by a hedgerow to a stile in
the fence beyond. Now walk beside the
river across a succession of narrow
pastures to a minor road (2h).

Turn left and stay with the road on a
vaguely upward drift for almost 1km to a
stone stile by a gateway (SP Askham
Bridge). Skirt the edge of woods, picking
up a wall to the left. Follow this to the
edge of a conifer plantation and then bear

left, dropping to a gate into the
churchyard. Descend, passing squat St
Peter's (the work of the same architect as
the castle) to reach the road. Make the
brief detour right to the river bridge
before heading uphill with the road back
into Askham (2h30).

'Almost an emperor, not quite a gentleman'

So said Edward VII of Hugh Cecil Lowther (1857-1944), the 5th Earl of Lonsdale. A paradigm of aristocratic
profligacy, Lonsdale dissipated the vast family fortune (one of the biggest in the country) in a blaze of
extravagance and bad management. Show-off, bon vivant and socialite, he was described as 'England's
greatest sporting gentleman': think of boxing's Lonsdale Belt, of chairing Arsenal Football Club, of
founding the National Sporting Club and of a passion for the Turf. His nickname, the 'Yellow Earl',
originated in his distinctive livery, which, as one of its founders and first president, he bestowed upon the
Automobile Association (AA). Predictably, it was under his watch that the castle was abandoned in 1936.
Twenty years later his great-nephew, the 7th Earl, removed the roof and sold off the materials.

Steel and steam

▲ Steel Knotts (432m)

Distance 7km **Time** 2 hours 30 (+ return trip by steamer between Glenridding and Howtown – 35 minutes each way)
Height gain 345m **Map** OS Explorer OL5
Access sandwich the walk with a return sailing on one of the excellent Ullswater 'Steamers' (they are all diesel nowadays) between Glenridding and Howtown. Glenridding is served by the 108 bus service from Penrith, the 208 Ullswater Connexion from Keswick (May-August) and the 517 Kirkstone Rambler from Windermere (March-October)

Everyone knows the Ullswater Steamer walk from Howtown to Patterdale – part classic, part cliché and painfully congested. How about a more intimate view of the country above the southern shore, leaving that bustling ribbon to your fellow passengers? Strike out to the elegant low ridge of Steel Knotts and to its sleepy neighbour Fusedale – all with a return crossing of the lake to look forward to.

Start at the steamer landing, Howtown (GR443199). Walk right over the footbridge, taking the lane to the left after the second gate. Cross the road, pass left of the hotel and follow a metalled lane (go right at the fork) up to a concrete farm track at the mouth of Fusedale.

Ascend by the wall to the right (SP Martindale Hause) to level ground, where a concrete water company post marks the beginning of the path (which appears to be no more than a sheeprun) up Steel Knotts. Initially an exercise in twisting steeply between rock protrusions and bracken, the path gains an easing gradient and drifts just west of the developing nose. It is a sparkling ascent – constantly engaging across folds and rises, past a cairned false summit and over too soon at a fine rock tor, the splendidly named

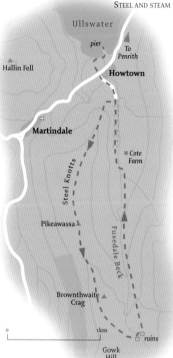

The saviour of the steamers

He is best known as a 'Boys' Own' figure, crucial in the development of English rugby union – he evolved a new style of forward play, captained his country to back-to-back Grand Slams, and chaired the RFU – but Baron Wakefield of Kendal (1898-1983), Wavell Wakefield, or 'Wakers' as he was affectionately known, was also the saviour of the steamers. In 1954, while a London MP, he acquired a controlling interest in the Ullswater Navigation and Transit Company, so saving the company. The following year he invited Donald Campbell to try Ullswater for his attempt to wrest back the water speed record, providing Campbell with a boathouse and slipway at Glenridding. The first of Campbell's records in Bluebird K7 was duly set on the lake on 23 July 1955.

Pikeawassa (GR440181) (1h).

Descend SSE to the saddle. Cross the wall and continue along the ridge, over a hummock, skirting right with the path around the non-descript top of Brownthwaite Crag. Descend slightly and then contour in a southeast-to-east arc over the coarse, and sometimes soggy, grass beneath Gowk Head to a pair of ruins (GR447169) (1h30). Bear north over a brief but often wet area to a firm green path leading across the narrow rowan-dotted cut of Groove Gill on a steep descent into the valley.

Wander along the valley bottom, staying right of Fusedale Beck. Approaching the intake wall and the footbridge over

Fusedale Beck, avoid the temptation to make a beeline for it – this leads into a peaty, saturated area. Instead, trend right to slightly higher ground before cutting down to the bridge further on. Now follow the concrete farm track north, past the point left at the beginning of the walk, and back by the outward route through Howtown to a hopefully shimmering Ullswater, and a 'steam' back to Glenridding (2h30).

◀ By Pikeawassa, a fine rock tor

19

The long way to Aira Force

▲ **Gowbarrow Fell** (481m)

Distance 6km **Time** 2 hours 30
Height gain 350m **Map** OS Explorer OL5
Access Aira Force car park and the nearby
Park Brow Foot are served by the 108 bus
service from Penrith and the 208
Ullswater Connexion from Keswick
(May-August)

The Victorians promoted the very
accessible charms of Aira Force
shamelessly, and today the beauty spot
is just as much on the tourist beat as it
ever was. But do not let that put you off,
for a couple of hours poking around
Gowbarrow Park, the rolling bracken-
and-heather upland to the east, brings
purpose and perspective to an outing
to one of the finest waterfalls in the
Lake District.

Start at Aira Force NT car park
(GR401200), just east of the junction of
the A592 and A509 by the north shore of
Ullswater. From the information boards
at the back of the car park, walk up the
tourist path to the falls. Bear right at the
first opportunity (through a break in the
metal fence), cross the footbridge over
Aira Beck and then keep right by another
fence as the path forks twice. Over a
stile, turn right along the base of the
open fell to a fork after 200m – take the
path left inclining to a high terrace
through heather and bracken. Contour
around to the stone memorial seat
('A Thank Offering 1905') with, just
below, the cairned top of Yew Crag, a
celebrated viewpoint over the lake.

Round the 'corner' to follow a
meandering line north along the eastern

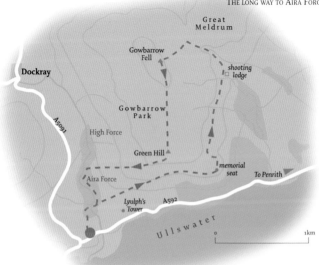

flank of Gowbarrow, twisting around rock outcrops and the incisions of gills on an enjoyable, undulating traverse to the crumbling walls of the 'shooting lodge' (GR414217).

Do not cross the ladder stile ahead and instead use the wall as a guide. Bear northwest, shadowing (at a distance) the wall and adjacent beck over some marshy and rough ground. As the wall bends WSW do likewise, following an intermittent path up the hummocky slope to the surprisingly craggy knoll topping Gowbarrow: it is capped by a trig point bearing an NT plaque (GR407218) (1h30).

Walk south across the open heathery plateau for 1km, traversing two smaller knolls en route to the cairned top of Green

Hill, another fine viewpoint. Descend sharply west by a thin green path to a stile close to the foot of the slope. Cross to the woods lining Aira Beck, turn downstream and fork right to the lower path (closer to the water). This is only in part a natural idyll – in the 19th century, the Howards of Greystoke Castle built the bridges and planted the specimens beside the falls to accentuate the Romantic appeal of the scene. The eastern bank offers all the happy exploring you need (a stone staircase leads down for a waterside view of the falls) and is the quieter of the two, though in mid-season it will not make much difference. Head downstream to return to the car park by the bridge crossed earlier (2h30).

◀ Sunset falls over the last steamer to Glenridding (from the memorial seat, Gowbarrow Park)

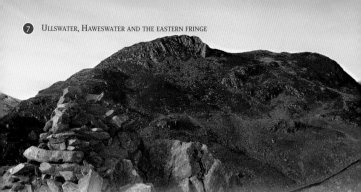

Glenridding divide

▲ Heron Pike (610m),
Glenridding Dodd (442m)

Distance 6km Time 2 hours 30
Height gain 495m Map OS Explorer OL5
Access Glenridding is served by the
108 bus service from Penrith, the 208
Ullswater Connexion from Keswick
(May-August) and the 517 Kirkstone
Rambler from Windermere
(March-October)

With open access to the fells, it is easy to
forget that much of the National Park
remains in private ownership. A rusting
reminder of this protrudes from Heron
Pike, one of Ullswater's finest
viewpoints, reached by an unusual and
varied route from Glenridding.

Start at the Lake District National Park
Authority (LDNPA) car park, Glenridding
(GR385169). Walk to the main road (A592)
and follow it north past the garage to the
edge of the village, dropping onto the
wooded path skirting Ullswater. The

constriction at Stybarrow Crag forces a
brief return to the road before resuming
above the shore for 500m to just beyond a
boathouse. Cross back over the A592 to a
private road (SP Seldom Seen, Glencoyne)
rising at the edge of broadleaf woods. After
500m, by a well-placed bench, note the
wonderful view back down the lake.

Just before the row of cottages, aptly
named Seldom Seen, branch onto a rough
stone path climbing to the left. The
gradient eases and a wall is joined to the
right for an easy tramp for 700m to a wall
running up/down the hillside (45 mins).
Cross the stile and then climb sharply up
the slope with the line of the wall. At a
point where the wall breaks left and begins
to descend, strike out right (southwest)
along a natural line of ascent just to the
left of a shallow, boulder-strewn chute.
Beyond this, gain the path up the steep
southeast ridge, climbing south of Heron
Pike to small tarns on level ground before
swinging east for 100m to the head of the

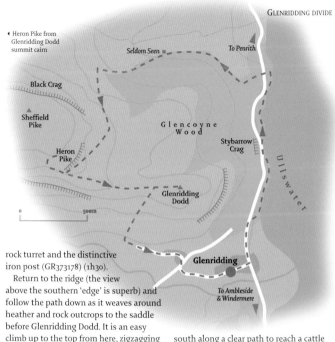

◄ Heron Pike from
Glenridding Dodd
summit cairn

Seldom Seen

To Penrith

Black Crag

Sheffield
Pike

Glencoyne
Wood

Stybarrow
Crag

Heron
Pike

Ullswater

Glenridding
Dodd

0   500m

Glenridding

To Ambleside
& Windermere

rock turret and the distinctive
iron post (GR373178) (1h30).

Return to the ridge (the view
above the southern 'edge' is superb) and
follow the path down as it weaves around
heather and rock outcrops to the saddle
before Glenridding Dodd. It is an easy
climb up to the top from here, zigzagging
first north then south, then rounding the
first knoll to a good summit cairn
(GR380175). Retrace the route back to the
saddle and descend the steep slope to the

south along a clear path to reach a cattle
grid by a row of cottages. Turn left down
the lane (Greenside Road) and then left
again at the T-junction to return to the
centre of the village (2h30).

'M' & 'H'

*The inscribed iron post above Heron Pike was set in 1912 to mark the boundary between the estates of
two landed families, the Marshalls of Patterdale Hall and the Howards of Greystoke Castle, near
Penrith. Despite the wartime requisition of the 3000-acre Greystoke Estate – the castle employed as a
prisoner of war camp, the surrounding land as a training area for tank drivers – the Howards are still
going strong, with the fourteenth generation of the family currently residing in the castle. Patterdale
Hall, on the other hand, is today an outdoor pursuits centre managed by Bolton School, with the
grounds and peripheral buildings of the estate dedicated, as is the way of things, to self-catering
holiday accommodation.*

A Grisedale excursion

Distance 9km **Time** 2 hours 15
Height gain 190m **Map** OS Explorer OL5
Access Patterdale is served by the 108 bus service from Penrith, the 208 Ullswater Connexion from Keswick (May-August), and the 517 Kirkstone Rambler from Windermere (March-October)

To be within the mountains is sometimes as rewarding as to be on the mountains. Never more so than in spindly Grisedale, a high-sided valley bathed in the wild romance dripping from the names around – Striding Edge, Eagle Crag, Pinnacle Ridge: perfect for a lazy day or a rainy day.

Start at the footpath in front of the Patterdale Hotel (GR395159). Walk right of the hotel into the small wood to the rear and up to a stile. Cross to a larger path inclining right between rock outcrops and bracken. Pick up a wall to the right (a companion for just over the next 1.5km) and traverse the fellside through Glenamara Park: cross the indent of Hag Beck and round the foot of the next ridge, Thornhow End. Undulate gently upwards by trees (pass to the right a path into the valley) and then down across open country into Grisedale proper. Continue, with only an intermittent path but the wall a reassuring presence, to a gate out onto the valley track.

Make for the head of the valley, passing Elmhow Farm and pine woods for superb views to the arc of surrounding mountains, from Dollywaggon Pike to Helvellyn. Then, 100m beyond the

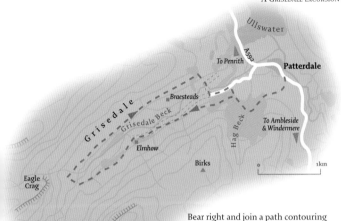

withdrawal of the wall to the right, branch to a footbridge leading over Grisedale Beck (GR362143). Rock is everywhere, from the high forbidding crags and the deep hollows either side of Nethermost Pike's east ridge to the stubby cone of Eagle Crag in the foreground. Follow the stony path away from the beck for 150m to a large boulder (1h15).

Bear right and join a path contouring along the base of the open fell for an easy stroll back down the valley. Pass above the farm at Braesteads and continue to the left of a wall for a further 600m. Coming to a gate ahead, turn through one to the right and descend to a track leading back over the beck and up to the road. Turn down the road, passing woods, for 375m to a path climbing the field to the right. Rise the short way into Glenamara Park and turn left, rejoining the path from the beginning of the walk. Retrace the way back over Hag Beck's stepping stones and into Patterdale (2h15).

The Lakes: as seen on TV

As of its time as Britpop and a belief in Tony Blair, the 1990's BBC television series The Lakes never shied from controversy during its brief run. Written by the hard-hitting one-time Grasmere resident Jimmy McGovern, here was a Lake District of wet slate grey, itinerant kitchen workers, adultery, kidnap and murder. Filmed in and around Patterdale and Glenridding with barely a daffodil in sight, the bleak narrative charted the descent into tortured guilt of Danny – an escapee from the city with poetic yearnings and dreams of release, played by a youthful John Simm – following a fatal accident upon Ullswater. The promoters of the twinkling lake and teashop vision of the Lakes were not happy.

◄ Nethermost Pike and Helvellyn soaring above Grisedale

Pioneering spirit

▲ St Sunday Crag (841m),
Gavel Pike (784m), Birks (622m)

Distance 11km **Time** 4 hours 15
Height gain 750m **Map** OS Explorer OL5
Access Patterdale is served by the 108 bus
from Penrith, the 208 Ullswater
Connexion from Keswick (May- August),
and the 517 Kirkstone Rambler from
Windermere (March-October)

**Connect with your pioneering spirit on
St Sunday Crag's empty eastern flank,
a superb alternative to Patterdale's
established high ascents.**

Start at the Patterdale Hotel (GR395159).
Walk south (past the general store) along
the A592 for 150m, then over the bridge on
the left and up the side road to a walled lane
on the right (SP Hartsop). Meander south
by the lane through the farms at
Crookabeck and Beckstones and the sparse
but charming wood between the
two. Bear right at the fork 200m
beyond Beckstones and
descend to a bridge. Leave the

track after 125m for a footpath splitting
right through the fields to the A592 at
Deepdale Bridge.

Cross to a walled lane opposite, which
almost immediately bends sharply right
towards the cottages at Lane Head. Just
below these, turn left onto a track leading
initially through bucolic pastures to
behind Deepdale Hall, then by a wall along
the foot of the fellside to above the farm at
Wall End. Leave the track as it turns down
to the farm, continuing ahead on a
footpath by the wall. Immediately past
Coldcove Gill, turn right to a large and
intricate sheepfold (GR391135) (1h).

A green path weaves up through bracken
to the left of the gill, then moves south to a
shoulder behind Latterhow Crag. The grassy
bowl wrapped around Gavel Moss and the
upper tributaries of Coldcove Gill opens
into view – the line of ascent follows the
rockier southern edge, moving west over a
low ridge to the subsidiary tops of Lord's
Seat and Gavel Pike. With the path fading
into an intermittently discernible trod, walk
briefly south along the level, then turn
southwest up the developing ridge. Rise
over forgiving grass to an area of shattered
crags 100m higher. Bear west to Lord's
Seat, picking a way around the large
shards of rock piercing the

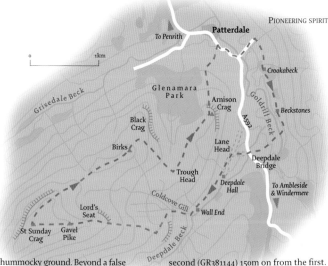

hummocky ground. Beyond a false summit the rock peters out and the gradient eases to leave a rough grass slope to the plain top of the knoll.

Cross an open shoulder WSW to the handsome pyramid of Gavel Pike. A steep path of sorts re-emerges west with some easy scrambling to the summit (GR373134). Continue west over a wide, shallow saddle to the lunar desolation of the cairn and shelter-dotted summit of St Sunday Crag (GR369134) (2h30).

Marked by a line of cairns, the gentle descent to the north soon gives way to much steeper ground and a twisting route broken by low eroded crags and exposed rock. Coming to a peaty col at 600m, the terrain shifts back to soft moorland folds – branch right, bearing ENE on a narrow path across a coarse grass spur, Birks. This is featureless other than for the twin mounds at the top, the

second (GR381144) 150m on from the first.

Some 100m past the second mound, dip right to locate the top of a wall (collapsed in its upper stages) running steeply down the eastern flank. Make a sharp descent to the right of this (pass south of the sheer crag two-thirds of the way down), to pick up a slim path skirting the top of the combe to Trough Head. Cross the trough itself and gain a path undulating northeast. Ride one distinct knoll, crossing the depression beyond to the foot of a larger and rockier one, Arnison Crag. There is the option here of either a quick scrambling traverse of the crag or of taking the path round to the west. Shadow the wall to the left (either here or further north if completing the traverse) for a guided, albeit steep descent to a large path contouring above the village. Turn right, then take the second kissing gate on the left to join a wooded path leading back to the hotel (4h15).

◀ Shards of rock breaking the grassy ascent to Lord's Seat

Twin peaks

▲ Angletarn Pikes (567m)

Distance 10.5km **Time** 3 hours 45
Height gain 525m **Map** OS Explorer OL5
Access Cow Bridge is served by the 517
Kirkstone Rambler from Windermere
(March-October). The 108 from Penrith
and the 208 Ullswater Connexion from
Keswick (May-August) both terminate at
Patterdale, 3km to the north

**Height snobs are apt to look down
(sometimes quite literally) upon
middling fells such as Angletarn Pikes.
Which is really their loss, for the union of
its twinned peaks to the graceful Angle
Tarn makes for a magical encounter,
particularly so on the traverse from
Hayeswater to Boredale Hause.**

Start at Cow Bridge car park off the A592
between Patterdale and the Kirkstone
Pass (GR403133). Walk southeast by the
main road for 250m, then branch left

along the side road to Hartsop. Follow the
road up to and through the charmingly
higgledy-piggledy village, forking right at
the head to a small car park. Follow the
signs for Hayeswater, joining a track rising
through open country to the left of
Hayeswater Gill. Beyond a cattle grid,
branch right with a track over the beck,
then turn uphill in line with the water,
cutting across the foot of Gray Crag. Carry
on into the narrow valley tightly
sandwiched between Gray Crag and The
Knott, remaining west of the gill up to the
bridge over the outlet from Hayeswater,
a natural lake channelled to supply
Penrith (GR428125).

From the tip of the lake, climb northeast
up a steepening and rather dull grass
slope, gaining close to its top a clear path
descending off The Knott. Join this,
contouring northwest around the peaty
flank of Rest Dodd. Pick up a fence to the

left, shadow it around a bend to the west, then deviate right to the enjoyably rugged top of the unseen Satura Crag, plunging into Bannerdale. The view north over the basin at the head of the valley is superb. Rejoin the path and drop down to the eastern edge of Angle Tarn (2h15).

Carry on round to just past a gill at the northern tip of the tarn and then ascend left of the gill by a thin path leading into the hollow behind the southern pike. Climb the short, steep slope left to the top, and then cross the hollow to scramble up to the top of the northern, and slightly higher, pike (GR413148).

Descend east along a faint path, soon meeting another running NNW down the gentle grassy slope to Boredale Hause. From the Hause, walk west by Stonebarrow Gill to join a good path raking steeply south into the valley. Reaching level ground the path merges into a track running south for 600m to a gated and walled lane. Follow this lane, remaining with it as it morphs into a ruler-straight metalled road. At the T-junction, turn right and then follow the main road the short way back to Cow Bridge (3h45).

◀ Hayeswater

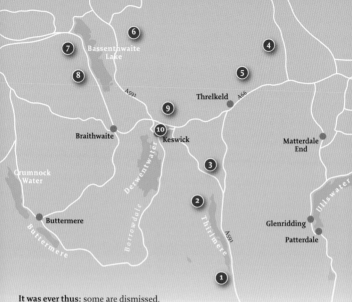

It was ever thus: some are dismissed, and some are cherished. Thirlmere is often dismissed: somewhere to pass through en route to somewhere else. But look closer and a century's worth of moss and lichen has softened the landscape, trees have grown and trees have fallen, nature has accommodated the man-made and vice versa. Walk up from the twisty western shore (or through the close by, low-key valley of St John's in the Vale) to find an earthy calm that is as surprising as it is refreshing.

There is an enjoyable hint of the undiscovered throughout these hills, from Bannerdale and the wickedly steep Barf to the hidden Wythop Valley. Of course, undiscovered is a word that could never be used about the cherished Blencathra and

Skiddaw. If one lives up to its reputation (slender-crested Blencathra, an exercise in honed, skeletal rock), the other perhaps does not (puffy old Skiddaw). So re-fashion the Skiddaw experience, first through Southerndale and then by the ridge of its elegant foothills.

Keswick is *the* walkers' centre in the Lakes. As a hub it is unrivalled, a practical base for this chapter, the next and for the one after that. Perhaps that is why it feels as if a shadow is sometimes cast over the walking from the front door. To see why that is unfair, start out on the old railway line to the Glenderaterra Valley, or perhaps just explore the environs of the town.

THIRLMERE, KESWICK AND THE NORTHERN HILLS

To the Beacon

▲ **The Beacon** (400m)

Distance 4km **Time** 1 hour 30
Height gain 230m **Map** OS Explorer OL5
Access the 555 bus service between
Keswick and Lancaster stops on the
A591 by Wythburn Church, 1.25km from
Steel End

Here is an antidote to all those who
dismiss Thirlmere: a beautiful short
walk from the edge of the water, flirting
with woods and up to a wonderful
viewpoint. Natural or unnatural – you
won't really care.

Start at Steel End car park, 500m up
from the southern end of the minor road

rounding the western shore of Thirlmere
(GR320129). Walk along the path from the
back of the car park, by the sign for
Dobgill. This leads towards the reservoir,
settling on a line just inland rather than
next to the water – save for a notable pine-
scattered headland with a terrific view
down the length of the water.

After 1km, by a network of mossy walls
serving no apparent purpose (perhaps a
legacy of the pre-flooding days), move up
with the path to a kissing gate to the road.
Turn right along the road then left after
100m into Dob Gill car park. Take the
pitched path rising ahead into the
conifers. Weave up to a steep section right

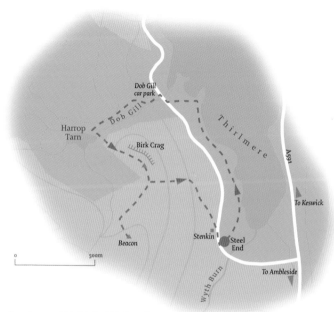

Harrop Tarn

Dob Gill car park

Dob Gill

Thirlmere

Birk Crag

A591

To Keswick

Stenkin

Steel End

Beacon

Wyth Burn

To Ambleside

0   500m

of a rock pyramid, behind which there is a good outlook over the waterfalls. More or less level ground leads from here through a young plantation to the marshy Harrop Tarn, set beneath crags. Bear left to cross the footbridge over the outlet then take the main path ahead for 100m to a deer gate on the left. Go through this and rise beside a rough wall to the modest head of Birk Crag, which reveals the view east.

Descend a short way south to a gate by a sheepfold, joining a green path beyond leading through one of the gaps in the tail of wall to the left. Continue south on a delightful green path to a bield, then cross left over the moss to a rocky knoll, at the top of which the beacon – more of a short wall than a cone – is easily made (GR314130). Backtrack down the knoll, over the moss and down the path to the tail of wall. Branch right to negotiate a sharp descent to the right of a wall, largely over rough but stable scree. Reaching a ruin on level ground, bear right, turning down through a farmyard to reach the road. Turn right to complete the circuit back to Steel End (1h30).

On the precipice (of Thirlmere)

▲ Raven Crag (461m)

Distance 6.5km Time 2 hours 15
Height gain 290m Map OS Explorer OL4
Access the 555 bus service between
Keswick and Lancaster follows the A591,
passing 150m east of Bridge End Farm

Raven Crag rises from Thirlmere's
conifers like a scaled-down version of
Yosemite's Half Dome. Wind through the
forest to the panoramic outlook at its
head, and then discover the ancient fort
of Castle Crag above the remote
Shoulthwaite Gill.

Start at the triangular parking area at the
western end of Thirlmere Dam (GR306189).
Walk north on the road for 100m to a thin
path rising left into the forest (SP Castle
Crag). Twisting enjoyably around natural
obstacles, the path soon leads to a much
wider, gently-graded path (perhaps once a
forestry road). Bear left along this towards
the now visible face of Raven Crag, which

suggests a far more intimidating ascent to
its top than it is. From close to the base of
the rock, loop around a bend to the
northwest, then 200m on (opposite a tall,
thin gate concluding a shortcut across the
zigzag just walked) break left up a narrow
path weaving steeply between trees.

Emerging at a partially cleared shoulder,
fork left through a dense, coniferous
tunnel by a large green sign. A gnarled
route now twists around trunks and
outcrops, over roots, up a stepped section
and across patches of duck boarding. The
barely marked summit of Raven Crag is
soon reached, with spectacular views east
over the length of the Thirlmere valley
(GR303187).

Return to the shoulder and take a path
leading west (SP Castle Crag) across a
forestry road, through a knot of trees and
over a beck to the compact rounded top of
Castle Crag, an ancient fort, a history
hinted at only by its formidable location

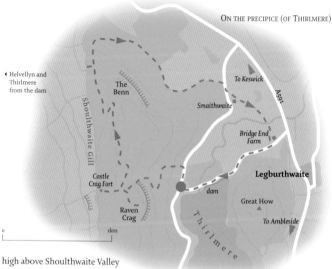

◄ Helvellyn and
Thirlmere
from the dam

The Benn

Shoulthwaite Gill

Castle Crag Fort

Raven Crag

To Keswick

A591

Smaithwaite

Bridge End Farm

Legburthwaite

dam

Great How

To Ambleside

Thirlmere

0   1km

high above Shoulthwaite Valley
(1h15). Walk back to the forestry road just
crossed and bear north (left), beginning a
gradual, slowly-opening descent.

Back on level ground, make the short
detour left to a bridge over Shoulthwaite
Gill: a charming, unfrequented corner of
the National Park and a pleasant place to
dawdle and rest. Return to the track and
continue north, staying with it around the
foot of the ridge and southeast past the
forlorn wetland of Shoulthwaite Moss.
Through a gate fork right to the road, then
right again along the asphalt and left into
the field after 100m (SP Footpath). Pass
between the barns – one an especially
handsome whitewashed example from
1692 – and descend to the beck, crossing
this at the footbridge. Walk up to and
through Bridge End Farm to the road.
Turn right to return to the parking area,
enjoying first a crossing of the curving
neo-gothic drama of Thirlmere Dam,
bookended by blasted crags (2h15).

A reservoir among the Lakes

*Open a tap in Manchester and chances are what flows out will come from Thirlmere. As the grand
tablet on the dam trumpets, the reservoir was a project of the Manchester Corporation and a matter of
some civic pride for its good burghers. Canon Rawnsley, soon to co-found the National Trust, took an
opposing view, combining with old friend John Ruskin in a failed bid to save the valley's soon-to-be-
flooded village and tarns. Work eventually began on the dam in 1890, although it was not until 1894
that the 154km (96-mile) aqueduct to Manchester was finally connected. Every day, around 220 million
litres of water leave the treatment works 5km south of the reservoir.*

In search of St John's

▲ **High Rigg** (357m)

Distance **8km** Time **2 hours 30**
Height gain **220m** Map **OS Explorer OL5**
Access **the 555 bus service between
Keswick and Lancaster follows the A591**

**When cloud obscures the higher fells,
break the longueur with an undulating
traverse of low-lying High Rigg, returning
from a secluded church through bucolic
St John's in the Vale.**

Start at Legburthwaite car park, which
is just north of Thirlmere off the B5322
(GR318195). From the gate at the rear of
the car park, walk left by the old road to
the A591 and then right along the verge
to a ladder stile just past the bridge.
Join a gently winding upward path,
forking directly up the slope after 100m.
A reasonably brief and steep ascent passes
between pines to the top of the first spur,
Wren Crag, where the falls and rises of the
ridge are revealed.

Dip through a hollow and follow a
rugged crest of knolls and outcrops –
entertaining but easy. Beyond a stile,
move away from the obvious path,
ascending with the fence to find a small
tarn. Descend left (northwest) into a bowl,
crossing a ladder stile by a junction of
walls. Shadow the wall to the right into a
trough between domed crags, then arc left
around a sodden depression and return to
the wall, continuing up a further rise.
Beyond the wall end, remain north to the
rocky summit crown (GR308220) (1h15).

Drop to the north over a springy,
steepening slope. Round the residential
youth centre to the left and walk right
down the road (a call at the church is

◄ The Church of St John's in the Vale

recommended), bearing off beyond the churchyard to a raking bridleway, once the principal route to the church for the communities to the south. Clinging to a lower wall, first in descent and then along the rolls of a charming terrace above the valley floor, the solid path sweeps south through pastoral tranquillity. (Note ahead Castle Rock, the prominent rock tower by the mouth of the valley.) Pass through two gates; 200m after the second – just beyond a walled, tree-shaded section – go through the gate ahead to the tiny Sosgill Bridge across the field.

Stay on the western bank and follow the levee upstream to Low Bridge Farm. Deviate to the right around the farmhouse and then drop to a good path leading beneath Wren Crag back to the side of the water. Rise right into woods to gain an elevated line above the beck, rounding the foot of the upland to rejoin the path down to the A591. Re-cross the bridge and return to Legburthwaite by the old road (2h30).

The Church of St John's in the Vale

The setting for the Church of St John's in the Vale must be the most isolated in the Lake District – and a contender for most charming. This was not always such a quiet spot, for the pass upon which it sits was once an important route linking the communities of St John's with Keswick and the west. The present building dates from 1845, though the site has reputedly been a place of worship since the 16th century. Blessed with a rustic simplicity, the church benefited from the remodelling of Crosthwaite Church in the latter part of the 19th century, inheriting from there both an alter by Sir George Gilbert Scott and wall panelling.

The Bannerdale bowl

▲ Bannerdale Crags (683m)

Distance 8km **Time** 2 hours 45
Height gain 460m **Map** OS Explorer OL5
Access Mungrisdale is connected to
Keswick at weekends by the 73/73A
Caldbeck Rambler

**Crag connoisseurs will revel in this ascent
of the rough east ridge of Bannerdale
Crags and the stride around the rim of an
impressively deep and rocky bowl.**

Start at Mungrisdale Recreation Rooms
(GR363302). Walk north by the road for
100m, then turn left down the stony lane
by the telephone box. Through the gate at
the end, join a stony path through open
country towards the jutting spur of The
Tongue. Cross a tiny footbridge and then,
sticking to the riverside, fork left at the
junction 50m on.

Stay with the Glenderamackin for
almost 1km, to just after the confluence
with subsidiary Bannerdale Beck.
Now bear right up a grassy slope to
gain the gently rising east ridge of
Bannerdale Crags, a sedate amble that
terminates abruptly at a scarred and
craggy face.

A stiff but entertaining ascent ensues,
around low crags and over some loose
stone, becoming a scramble in the upper
and middle ranges, though there are
no particular difficulties. With barely a
transition, the face suddenly gives
way to reveal an innocuous, rounded
upland. Trend slightly right (west) to
locate the modest summit cairn
(GR335290) (1h30). From here, a detour
100m southwest opens a great view
to Blencathra.

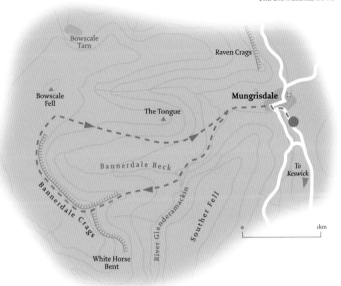

Back at the summit, follow the spectacular rim of the crags on an arc to the north. Before the rise to Bowscale Fell, join a wide path ESE, raking ruler-straight down the southern flank of The Tongue.

With an easing gradient, the path merges into a loose track – follow this around the base of the ridge to the footbridge crossed earlier. Now trace the outward route back into sleepy Mungrisdale (2h45).

Lake District National Park

Mungrisdale lies almost on the boundary of the Lake District National Park – to one side of the village rise the high fells, to the other falls away the wide plain of the Eden Valley. The idea of creating National Parks in Britain took hold in the 1920s as pressure built to ensure both the preservation of – and open access to – Britain's wildest and most beautiful landscapes. The movement gathered pace through the mass trespasses of the 1930s and the Dower Report of 1945, which supported the National Park concept. Finally, in 1949, Attlee's government passed the National Parks and Access to the Countryside Act, described by Lewis Silkin, the then Minister of Town and Country Planning, as "the most exciting act of the post-war parliament", which was saying something. In 1951, the Lake District was duly designated one of the country's four original National Parks and – until the creation of the Cairngorms National Park in 2003 – the biggest at 2214 sq km.

◄ Bannerdale Crag's east ridge rising beyond The Tongue

Blencathra ridges

▲ Blencathra (868m)

Distance 7km **Time** 3 hours 30
Height gain 690m **Map** OS Explorer OL5
Access Threlkeld is connected to Keswick
and Penrith by the hourly X4/X5 bus service

*NB: Under snow and ice, Hall's Fell Ridge is a
suitable destination for experienced and properly
equipped mountaineers only*

**Ride a jagged alpine ridge straight to the
summit of this iconic mountain, then
descend by its towering neighbour – a
spectacular round for lovers of thrills
(but beware the spills).**

Start at Blease Road car park, Threlkeld
(GR318256). Take the path from the car
park entrance rising towards the fell. Cross
a footbridge over tree-lined Kilnhow Beck
and continue in line with the stream up to
a gate through the intake wall. Turn right,
shadowing the wall along the bottom of
Gategill Fell, the second of the five
buttresses constituting the magnificent
south face of the mountain. Cross the
forded bed of the usually dried-up Gate
Gill, the violent gash dividing Gategill Fell
and Hall's Fell, directly above which the
summit may be seen. Here, you begin to
ascend the ridge.

The first section of Hall's Fell has a
consistent grinding steepness, but the
route – along a series of small, clearly
defined zigzags through heather, rock and
grass – is obvious enough. The path drifts
towards the eastern side before turning
back sharply to the centre of the fell, the
gradient easing as the sense of height and
air develops. A rock knoll at 620m marks
the beginning of Narrow Edge (1h15). From
here, the ridge rises as a sequence of
fractured stone turrets between grass
terraces. An easy path skirts the eastern
side, but it is much more enjoyable and
rewarding to scramble over the rock along
the crest. Indeed, one of the best aspects
of the ridge is the extent to which it is
possible to make the route as hard or easy

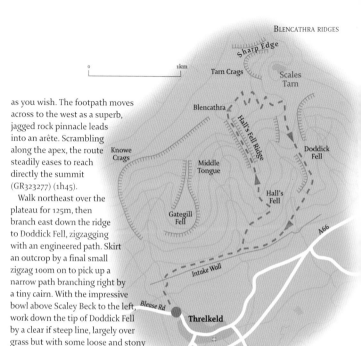

as you wish. The footpath moves across to the west as a superb, jagged rock pinnacle leads into an arête. Scrambling along the apex, the route steadily eases to reach directly the summit (GR323277) (1h45).

Walk northeast over the plateau for 125m, then branch east down the ridge to Doddick Fell, zigzagging with an engineered path. Skirt an outcrop by a final small zigzag 100m on to pick up a narrow path branching right by a tiny cairn. With the impressive bowl above Scaley Beck to the left, work down the tip of Doddick Fell by a clear if steep line, largely over grass but with some loose and stony sections, though nothing to rival Hall's Fell. In the middle ranges, the views back to the apparently conical summit are excellent, particularly so from the level top of the lower spur, two-thirds of the way down. From here the winding path trends towards the Doddick Gill side, meeting the

intake wall just east of the gill. Bear right, round the gill and then contour with the intake wall across the pastoral lower slopes of Hall's Fell. Back at Gate Gill, retrace the outward route to Threlkeld (3h30).

Shock and awe

Considered wild, primitive and dangerous, the mountains of the Lake District were regarded with awe by adventurous travellers intent on feeding the Romantic imagination. In The History of Cumberland (1794), William Hutchinson recounts how a party of three gentlemen fared in an attempt to scale Blencathra the preceding year. Though their guide led one successfully to the summit, one was 'suddenly taken ill', wishing to 'lose blood and return', while the third 'was so astonished at the different appearance of the objects in the valley that he declined proceeding'.

◂ One summit, two ridges: Blencathra, Hall's Fell Ridge (left) and Doddick Fell (right)

Skiddaw foothills

▲ **Longside Edge** (734m),
Ullock Pike (692m)

Distance 8.5km **Time** 3 hours 30
Height gain 600m **Map** OS Explorer OL4
Access the infrequent 73/73A and 554/555
bus services follow the A591 through
High Side

**Leave the dull tourist routes up Skiddaw
for the crowds. Extract the best of the
mountain (with just sheep for company)
on a sweep through Southerndale to
Carlside Col, returning along the graceful
spine of the Ullock Pike ridge, as ahead
the Lake District fades out into coastal
plains and the Solway Firth.**

Start at the small parking area on the
minor road to Orthwaite, 300m north of its
junction with the A591 at High Side
(GR236309). Walk a few metres uphill and
through the gate to the right (SP
Bridleway). Cross the beck and follow the
path towards a gate ahead. Veer off with

the hawthorns as they turn to rake across
the field, remaining in the same direction
for 100m past their end before ascending
left to a ladder stile. A green track
emerges, sweeping around the foot of the
ridge into the next field and, through
another gate, to above Southerndale Beck.
Remain with the track for a further 250m,
then drop down to cross the beck close to
a sheepfold.

Do not be tempted by the path heading
directly up the slope; instead, trend right
along quad bike tracks through a reedy and
potentially wet but small area to gain a
more defined route up the valley.
Originally a drove road, this is now
overgrown and receding gradually back
into the moor. Rise to a wide, shallow
basin, curving with the path around its
eastern side, beneath Buzzard Knott, in an
arc leading back to the south. Following

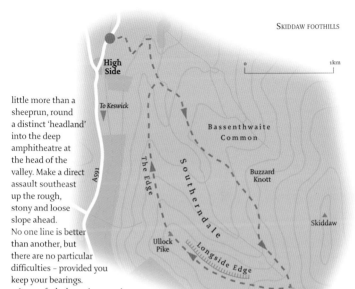

little more than a sheeprun, round a distinct 'headland' into the deep amphitheatre at the head of the valley. Make a direct assault southeast up the rough, stony and loose slope ahead. No one line is better than another, but there are no particular difficulties – provided you keep your bearings.

It may feel a long time coming, but the arrival at Carlside Col and its accompanying pool, the miserable Carlside Tarn, is sudden (GR255282) (1h45). From the tarn, take the right-hand path west, descending slightly before rising to airy Longside Edge, the apex of a narrow ridge (and on the Southerndale side a true edge). Roll first down and then briefly up to the fine rock cone of Ullock Pike

(GR244287), descending beyond along the lovely, undulating crest of The Edge. Press on over a saddle to the bouldery top of Watches and down to the intake wall. Shadow the wall right to the Southerndale track, turning left through the gate to retrace the way back to High Side (3h30).

'God made manifest'

At the height of his career in the 1970s and early '80s, 'enfant terrible' film director Ken Russell resided in Borrowdale, (at Coombe Cottage, 800m north of Grange off the B5289). How that came to be, he explained to The Guardian in October 2005: "In 1968, I was coming up to scout for locations for a film with Oliver Reed called Dante's Inferno *about the pre-Raphaelite founder Rossetti's personal crisis. I drove my Morris up 300 miles from Notting Hill to Keswick. I got there after dark and when I woke up in the morning and opened the curtains I looked across the lake and saw God made manifest: Skiddaw mountain. That's what Coleridge said when he first saw it – God made manifest." Russell went on to film sequences for* The Devils, Tommy *and* Women in Love *in the district.*

◀ Ullock Pike disappears into mist over Southerndale

A way through Wythop Woods

▲ Sale Fell (359m)

Distance 9km **Time** 2 hours 45
Height gain 400m **Map** OS Explorer OL4
Access The Pheasant Inn is served by the
seasonal 74/74A Osprey Bus from Keswick

**Smaller and altogether less visitor-
orientated than the Whinlatter Forest
Park just to the south, moody Wythop
Woods are much more appealing. Take a
trip off the beaten track, with twisty
routes in and out of the trees
sandwiching the hidden Wythop Valley
and the springy, rounded turf of Sale Fell.**

Start at The Pheasant Inn by
Bassenthwaite Lake (GR199307). Walk up
the minor road from the side of the hotel
towards the forest behind, branching left
by the sign for Peil Wyke onto a single-
track Forestry Commission road. After
250m, just as the road dips, look for a path
angling back on the right. Rise for 20m to
another path, following this left as it
opens into a green track passing above

disused quarry buildings. Turn uphill
on a much larger and more robust track,
bearing right at the first fork. Continue to
zigzag up the track, bearing straight off at
the fourth hairpin onto an overgrown
green lane clinging to the steep hillside.
Slimming to a path, this leads briefly
through a gloomy coniferous tunnel, then
into lighter trees before arriving at a gate
onto the open fell.

From the gate, either continue ahead by
the fence, or better cut directly up the
slope past patches of gorse, to reach a
charming path inclining gently southwest
above the somnolent Wythop Valley.
Follow the path into the natural
woodland of Chapel Wood, past the
melancholy remains of Wythop Old
Church and into open fields (1h15). At the
head of the farm road beyond Kelswick,
join a grassy rake rising WNW beneath
Dodd Crag. Approaching a wall, cut back
ENE, passing above the crag on an easing
slope. A clearly defined route now

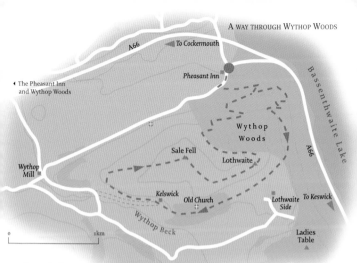

continues in the same direction over rounded slopes to the modest summit of Sale Fell (GR194296). Descend southeast to a gate and up a hardly perceptible gradient to a cairned subsidiary top, then bear ENE over a shallow depression and traverse the top of Lothwaite (GR202296) (2h) to the edge of the forest.

Turn left, tracking the boundary wall on a gently descending path to a gate. Cut right to a stile into the trees 150m beyond this; forge ahead for 50m to a soft track and walk downhill to where the track levels out. Before it begins to rise again, break left onto a path quickly bending back sharply left (west). After around 250m of gentle, arrow-straight descent look for a shortcut down to the next terrace and bear right. In approximately 200m, split left onto the path first ascended from the road. Follow this and the roads back to the many pleasures of The Pheasant (2h45).

The Bassenthwaite ospreys

When a pair of ospreys nested in Wythop Woods in 2001, it marked the return of the bird to the Lake District after a break of 150 years. One of the world's most spectacular birds, with a wingspan of up to 1.7m, the osprey was absent from Britain altogether between 1916 and the introduction of a breeding pair to Scotland in 1954. Local sightings of migratory flights during the late 1990s prompted the Forestry Commission and RSPB to build the nest platform that eventually proved successful. Since then the Bassenthwaite ospreys have returned every year to breed, in 2008 relocating their nest to the other side of the lake. They remain local celebrities with a designated viewing point ten minutes walk from the Mirehouse car park off the A591.

An audience with the Bishop

▲ Barf (460m), Lord's Seat (552m)

Distance 5km Time 2 hours 45
Height gain 485m Map OS Explorer OL4
Access Thornthwaite is served by
the X4/X5 bus service from Keswick
and Cockermouth

A walk and a scramble in equal measure
(and sprinkled with local folklore), this
direct approach to the oddly named Barf
is perhaps the steepest and most
adventurous route from the valley floor
in the Lakes.

Start at Powter How car park,
Thornthwaite (GR220265). Cross to the
minor road opposite and walk up to a
junction, turning right and then right
again through the gate some 50m on

(SP Footpath). Pass the whitewashed
stone of The Clerk, and ascend the steep
scree slope. This is not as hard as it looks
– the passage of feet has crafted a
reasonably stable line to the unmistakable
Bishop, while sporadic outbreaks of
vegetation provide useful cement.

Continue up into the gully above: the
line to the right is initially the best, with a
move to the left preferable once in it.
Either way, the rock is very flaky and not
to be trusted. Beyond, advance through
heather and bracken past a rowan tree to a
more solid patch of scree. At the small
crags, a cleft just right of centre leads up
to a steep heathery slope. After a few
metres, a wide zigzag can be executed on a
line worn through the heather – first right
and then back across yet more scree to an
oak and rowan together at the base of
crags. Trend left on a higgledy-piggledy

Who is the Bishop?
*While staying at The Swan Hotel in 1783, the
Bishop of Derry entered into a wager with the
proprietor that he could ride his horse up the
forbidding slope of Barf. It is said that the Bishop
rock marks the point where he fell and plunged
down the scree, the Clerk where his body came to a
rest. It became tradition for the staff of The Swan
to whitewash the rocks in his memory – given their
pristine appearance, someone has apparently
inherited the job now that the hotel is defunct.*

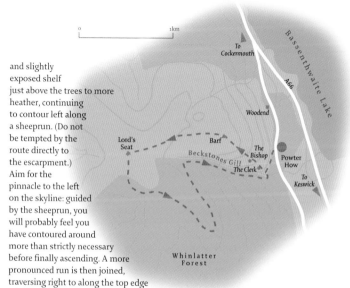

and slightly exposed shelf just above the trees to more heather, continuing to contour left along a sheeprun. (Do not be tempted by the route directly to the escarpment.) Aim for the pinnacle to the left on the skyline: guided by the sheeprun, you will probably feel you have contoured around more than strictly necessary before finally ascending. A more pronounced run is then joined, traversing right to along the top edge of the escarpment. Now weave uphill over an initial rise to near the top of a second knoll, where the main Beckstones path is reached. The summit of Barf is quickly gained from here (GR214267) (1h15).

Off the top, descend west to a boggy depression, continuing in the same direction over a firmer section to an eroded, peaty area. Through this, a stony path gives way to more peat on the final rise to the top of Lord's Seat (GR204265) (1h45). Descend a short way south to a stile, crossing to a constructed path. Follow this past intermittent trees to a fork by a marker post, bearing left into light woods. The path soon morphs into a forestry road leading back out of the trees.

After 150m turn left onto an apparently abandoned road: there is a good perspective back to the ascent here. Descend gradually north into a more mature plantation. Turn down the grassy track by Beckstones Gill, then, at the meeting with a contouring road, turn right, and then left after 100m to continue the descent. Drop in line with the gill to the only point of potential difficulty, an awkward rock step best taken by utilising a ledge running left to right. After this the gradient steepens into a thick knot of trees. Levelling out, take the path round to a stile opening to the road. Turn left, cross the ford and walk back along the road used at the start (2h45).

◀ The Bishop of Barf

North by Northeast

▲ Latrigg (368m)

Distance 15.5km **Time** 4 hours 30
Height gain 420m **Map** OS Explorer OL4

All aboard! Depart Keswick by the old railway line on an extended introduction to the valleys north and east – calling at the River Greta, the Glenderaterra Valley and Latrigg.

Start at the tourist information centre in the Moot Hall, Market Place, Keswick (GR266234). Walk up Station St and then Station Rd as it bisects Fitz Park, taking the sharp bend right on to Brundholme Rd before the former railway hotel. Stick with the road to just past the bridge over it, where steps to the right rise up the embankment to the railway path.

Walk east out of town, beneath the soaring arches and roaring traffic of Greta Bridge, (voted the Best Concrete Engineering Structure of the Century in September 1999) and over a strikingly attractive section of elevated boardwalk above the river. Now follow the largely tree-lined path for almost 2km, crossing three times over the meandering Greta.

By a stone shelter 100m before a fourth bridge, leave the path by the gate to the left. Cross the field to a metalled lane and turn uphill (1h15).

Just past a cottage follow the lane into woods and branch right onto a path. Descend to a footbridge over Whit Beck, rising on the far bank along an enclosed path between fields to the whitewashed farmhouse of Derwentfolds. Turn right up the drive and left after 150m (SP Footpath) onto a delightful green terrace gradually rising into the Glenderaterra valley.

After 1.4km, as the track begins to noticeably descend for the second time (above the crumbling ruins of a mine), incline diagonally up the slope along a reedy, overgrown but nevertheless faintly discernible rake. If this ceases to be clear, simply tramp NNE up rough grass to meet the main north-south path. Continue up the valley on this, over two tributaries and past a prominent sheepfold to a footbridge over Glenderaterra Beck (GR296278) (2h30). Cross and take the steepening path to a fork, bearing left for a short, steady climb to the fine route contouring across the steep eastern flank of Lonscale Fell.

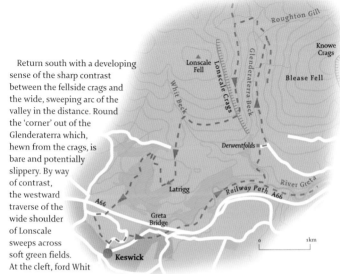

Return south with a developing sense of the sharp contrast between the fellside crags and the wide, sweeping arc of the valley in the distance. Round the 'corner' out of the Glenderaterra which, hewn from the crags, is bare and potentially slippery. By way of contrast, the westward traverse of the wide shoulder of Lonscale sweeps across soft green fields. At the cleft, ford Whit Beck, then keep with the path south. Pass to the east of Latrigg car park, taking the wide path beyond the fence ahead. Quickly veer off the improved path to pick up the fence to the left, shadowing this up an easing slope to level ground. Turn west upon meeting the obvious path running east-west over the felltop (GR278246) (3h45). Now descend gradually with the zigzags of the tourist route. At the path junction by the edge of the

conifers, turn down sharply to the left, where a well-blazed route drops towards Keswick through the woods, widening into Spooney Green Lane. Having crossed the bridge over the A66 to the edge of town, turn right down Briar Rigg, and then left after 200m, by the stump of a decapitated bridge, into Fitz Park. Follow the asphalt path past the cricket pitch back to Station Road. Turn right for the bright lights of Keswick (4h30).

The Cockermouth, Keswick and Penrith Railway

History has already thrown Dr Beeching, his report and the dark arts behind the savaging of Britain's railways into rogues' corner. Take the Cockermouth, Keswick and Penrith Railway: consider how practical to residents and appealing to visitors a regular train service linking the West Coast mainline, the Northern Lakes and West Cumbria would be today. Opened in 1865, it was 'death by a thousand cuts' for the 50km line post-Beeching, the last train running from Keswick to Penrith on Saturday 4 March 1972.

◀ Lonscale Fell and the Glenderaterra Valley

The long and short of Keswick

Distance 8km (short 4km) Time 2 hours 15 (short 1 hour 15) Height gain 90m (short 80m) Map OS Explorer OL4

Absorb one of the most strikingly set towns in England on a wander in and around the margins of Keswick, the bustling metropolis of the Northern Lakes. With a shorter option if refreshment beckons.

Start at the tourist information centre in the Moot Hall, Market Place, Keswick (GR266234). Walk along St John Street/Ambleside Road for 600m to the foot of a hill, turning right onto Springs Rd. After 150m, turn right down a narrow path to the handsome wooded cone of Castle Head, a former volcano. Climb the broad path (ignoring the two paths breaking right along the way) up to the rock platform at the top for a famed view over Derwentwater, its islands and surrounding fells (GR269226).

Return to the higher path ignored earlier (above the wall) and descend west to Borrowdale Rd, forking left above the road to the steps opposite the lane to Cockshot

Wood. Follow this into the trees, turning immediately left down a path within the edge of the woods to open ground. Follow a well-worn route to the lake shore, with Lord's Island directly ahead, and turn right, rounding the northern curve of Strandshag Bay to a rock promontory, Friar's Crag. Climb the steps to the Ruskin Memorial, a wedge of Borrowdale stone elegantly inscribed with a quote from the Victorian polymath's oeuvre. Continue onto a metalled lane leading past the new promenade and landing stages before curving away with the road.

Opposite the theatre entrance, take the gate into Crow Park, dip down to the shore and then shadow the scrubby, curving fringe of the field around to a gate at the edge of town. Walk by the road ahead, past the caravan site, the bus station and Booth's supermarket, to the mini-roundabout at the end of Tithebarn St. If cutting the walk short, cross right here to return to the Market Place.

Bear left along Main St, passing the Cumberland Pencil Works to the right, and turn left by the river after Greta Bridge.

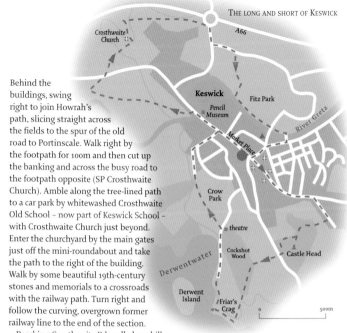

Behind the buildings, swing right to join Howrah's path, slicing straight across the fields to the spur of the old road to Portinscale. Walk right by the footpath for 100m and then cut up the banking and across the busy road to the footpath opposite (SP Crosthwaite Church). Amble along the tree-lined path to a car park by whitewashed Crosthwaite Old School – now part of Keswick School – with Crosthwaite Church just beyond. Enter the churchyard by the main gates just off the mini-roundabout and take the path to the right of the building. Walk by some beautiful 19th-century stones and memorials to a crossroads with the railway path. Turn right and follow the curving, overgrown former railway line to the end of the section.

Reaching Crosthwaite Rd, walk downhill for 125m, then cross left to a footpath shadowing Brundholme Rd. Just before the railway embankment turn right on a hard path into Fitz Park. Before the cricket pitch swing right to the riverside, walking beneath the bridge carrying Station Rd and on to Wivell footbridge over the Greta. Cross Penrith Rd and turn right, left down Station St and then finally right again by Keswick Lodge to return to the Moot Hall (2h15).

Cultural Keswick

In an area that trades rather too much on the distant legacy of the Lake Poets, Keswick has embraced a heartening contemporary cultural renaissance. Put that down, at least in part, to the wonderful Theatre by the Lake, opened in 1999. An incomparably better successor to the Century Theatre (the so-called Blue Box that occupied the same site from 1976 to 1996), the building houses a 400-seat auditorium, a 100-seat studio, two gallery spaces, meeting facilities, a coffee shop and bars. Home to a professional repertory company, the theatre also provides a venue for the Words on the Water Literary Festival (which nets some big fish), the Keswick Film Festival and Keswick Jazz Festival.

◀ A Keswick sunset

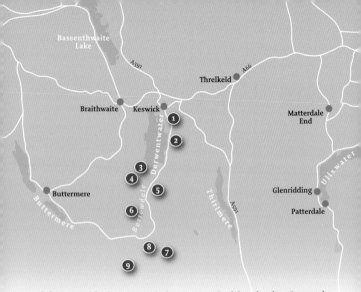

South from Keswick a journey unwinds: through the Vale of Derwentwater, into Borrowdale, and then down Langstrath or to Seathwaite, the fraying threads of the valley. The end comes with the rock and elemental forces of England's highest mountains. Consider it a journey into the wild.

It begins so politely. The Vale of Derwentwater, a palette of green and rust, loops around the twinkling 'Queen of the Lakes'. This was the Victorians' perfect country scene, a Romantic playground of striking vistas, natural curiosities, rustic bridges, stately woods and friendly fells. That gentility tempts and charms still, so embrace it, avoid the coach parties and seek out the few glimpses of a less-refined nature where you can, upon Nitting Haws, say.

South of chocolate-box Grange, the land is compressed and folded into the almost clenched Jaws of Borrowdale, a ravine with cascading crags, neat but haphazard peaks, sylvan bowers and a turquoise-reflected river. It is as if a vast scale replica had been made of some quaint alpine corner. The walking here is of abundant, concentrated variety, and is oddly appealing in the rain, when the showy gleam of beauty slips into an agreeable melancholy.

The shift further south, into a circle of rolling pastures, whitewashed villages and disarming tranquillity is as short as it is sudden. Then, past Rosthwaite, the mountains are all. Here, take up the lonely and overlooked challenges of Eagle Crag, Rosthwaite Fell and Great End.

DERWENTWATER, BORROWDALE AND THE CENTRAL FELLS

Derwentwater perspectives

▲ **Walla Crag** (379m), **Castle Head** (162m)

Distance 9km Time **2 hours 45**
Height gain **360m** Map **OS Explorer OL 4**

**Take in three celebrated outlooks over
Derwentwater on this classic round,
rising from the shoreline by Friar's Crag
to the bare top of Walla Crag. Return over
Castle Head, the stump of the volcano
that helped to shape the area.**

Start at Lake Rd car park, Keswick
(GR265229). Walk past the theatre to the
lake shore, following the lane past the
promenade and jetties to the wooded
peninsula of Friar's Crag, home to the
Ruskin memorial and a wide, watery view.
Arc with the shore into woods (The Ings)
on an obvious path, then out of the trees
bear right down the track to the cottages
at Stable Hills, rounding these to return
to the water. From a second wooded
peninsula (Broom Point), follow the
semicircle of Calfclose Bay – ignore the
path to the road by the NT collecting cairn
– to and around the next headland, rising
to Borrowdale Rd as the path comes to a
rocky finish.

Cross the road to a stile 20m right and
walk up from the boulders to gain a path
contouring across the slope. Turn left
towards Great Wood, shadowing the
perimeter wall up to the footbridge over Cat
Gill. Join a pitched path rising steeply to
the left of the beck, with occasional
zigzags. Clear of the trees, but before the
gradient has eased, leave the gill on a path
running to the right of a wall. Shadow the
wall NNE for 300m up easier, open ground
to a stile. Cross here and make the short
way to the top of Walla Crag, a sheet of
bare, fractured rock with a precipitous
view over Derwentwater, its islets, and the
scattered jumble of settlements, woods
and fells beyond (GR276213) (1h30).

Leave to the northeast to rejoin the
main wallside path beyond a second stile,

Keswick

250m on from the first. Descend in the same direction over a steepening grass slope to the micro-settlement of Rakefoot. Cross the footbridge and turn down the road, branching left after 200m (SP Keswick/Great Wood). Cross back over Brockle Beck and head downstream above tree-lined banks. Past the television mast, execute an 'S' bend with the path, first right to the wood, then left by the beck.

Walk through Springs Wood to its namesake farm, joining the road at Keswick's salubrious fringe. After 400m, turn left along the narrow path to the neatly domed Castlehead Wood. Climb the broad path, ignoring the two paths breaking right along the way, to the rock

platform at the top – Castle Head (GR269226). Return to the higher of the paths ignored earlier (before the wall) and descend west to Borrowdale Rd. Fork left above the road to the steps opposite the lane to Cockshot Wood. Entering the wood take the path ahead to return to the lake shore (2h45).

Lady's Rake

Just south of the top cuts the only breach in Walla Crag (though not a practicable means of ascent), Lady's Rake. The name derives from Jacobite folklore, when the Countess of Derwentwater is said to have scaled the deep gully to effect an escape following the capture of her husband, the 3rd Earl, a supporter of the rising. Treasure hunters may be interested to learn that en route from her home on Lord's Island her ladyship threw her copious jewels into the lake rather than allow them to be captured – or so it is claimed. One known fact is that the story does not end happily; for his troubles the Earl was executed in 1716 (aged 27), while the countess died in exile seven years later.

◀ Derwentwater jetties

One-way Borrowdale

Distance 11.5km **Time** 3 hours 30
Height gain 380m **Map** OS Explorer OL 4
Access Rosthwaite is served by the 78
Borrowdale Rambler

Postcard favourites Ashness Bridge and Watendlath spring to life on this linear tour through the rolling country along the eastern edge of the valley. At its best in winter or at the margins of the day, when the inevitable crowds thin.

Start at the tourist information centre in the Moot Hall, Market Place, Keswick (GR266234). Walk along St John St/Ambleside Road (right of the George Hotel) for 600m to the foot of a hill, turning right onto Springs Rd. Remain on the road to its end, passing left of Springs Farm, through a gate and into woods. Join a path beside Brockle Beck and, 250m on, turn right (SP

Rakefoot Farm) to a fenced path rising at the edge of the trees.

After 400m, take the path crossing right to the pines of Great Wood. A charming undulation through the upper reaches of the wood leads into a constant, raking descent for 700m. At a meeting of paths turn left, drifting gently upward to the footbridge over Cat Gill (1h). Cross and briefly drop by the wall to pick up a narrow path contouring through bracken beneath the magnificent Falcon Crag. Branching left at a fork (SP Ashness Bridge), weave upwards through more bracken and then gently descend to the road just below photographers' favourite Ashness Bridge.

Ascend by the road over the bridge and up the hill beyond, twisting through a series of bends past Ashness Cottage and

◀ Which way now? Direction stone by Watendlath Beck

Ashness Farm to the famous Surprise View, a sheer cliff just to the right of the road (GR268188). The surprise is perhaps that it lives up to its reputation – caution should be exercised. Split right, 100m on, to a thin, muddy path winding a short way between trees to a junction with a more developed path. Turn right, slanting down through woodland to a footbridge over Watendlath Beck. Cross the bridge and head upstream.

Watendlath Beck, the sometimes pitched path beside it, the narrow secluded valley, the scattered copses and the developing crags combine to make the next 2km a delight. Having moved away from the water in its latter stages, the path returns to the beck just before a gate into Watendlath itself. Go through this, turn right before the tarn, through a second gate and then fork right (SP Rosthwaite) up a loose stone track (2h45). Crest to a shoulder of open fell, passing south of Puddingstone Bank for a steady, eroded descent, with some exposed rock and an excellent outlook over Rosthwaite and Borrowdale. As the gradient eases to a more-or-less level terrace, look for a gate to the right (SP Public Bridleway Rosthwaite) for a direct descent of the final field. Locate the gate by trees in the southwest corner and walk down the walled lane beyond. Opposite

the entrance to Hazel Bank, turn right over the bridge across Stonethwaite Beck to the edge of Rosthwaite – the bus stop, and the promise of an open deck ride back to Keswick, is across the road (3h30).

The bays of Derwentwater

Distance 6km **Time** 1 hour 30 (+ launch)
Height gain 40m **Map** OS Explorer OL4
Access for the likely scenario of
beginning in Keswick, take the clockwise
sailing to Lodore, completing the journey
in the same direction from High
Brandelhow. Sailings leave every hour,
more frequently at the height of
summer, with both the outward and
return legs taking 20 minutes

**From Brandelhow Mine to the Lodore
Hotel and the studied beauty of
Brandelhow Park, trace a journey through
the area's Victorian transition from
industry to tourism and preservation,
finishing by perhaps the finest section of
lake shore in the National Park.**

Start at the Lodore landing stage
(GR264192). Walk to the road and turn
right, past the hotel, over the brow and on
to a gate on the right after a further 100m
(SP Manesty). Wander down the wide,
recently-hardened footpath to cross the

River Derwent at Chinese Bridge, then
follow a section of duckboarding to a
swing gate, resuming on firm ground with
views of Maiden Moor and Catbells ahead.
Negotiate two shorter sections of
duckboarding. At the end of the second,
take a narrow green path splitting right to
a lonely headland which has a wonderful
view down the length of the lake, a sort of
reverse Friar's Crag. Continue around the
headland to a stile by Myrtle Bay, rejoining
the main path beyond.

Entering wooded Manesty Park, the
path cuts behind the next headland to the
shore at Abbot's Bay and on, away from
the water for 150m, to a junction of paths
by a low cottage, The Warren. Turn right
down the track, then bear left at the fork
to a whitewashed cottage. Cross the
shingle bay to a swing gate, rounding the
spoilheaps, a remnant of the long-defunct
Brandelhow Mine, to High Brandelhow
landing stage (GR251197).

Take the path inclining away from the

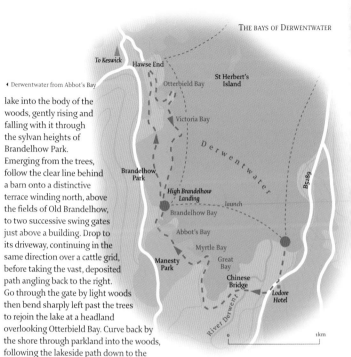

◄ Derwentwater from Abbot's Bay

lake into the body of the woods, gently rising and falling with it through the sylvan heights of Brandelhow Park. Emerging from the trees, follow the clear line behind a barn onto a distinctive terrace winding north, above the fields of Old Brandelhow, to two successive swing gates just above a building. Drop to its driveway, continuing in the same direction over a cattle grid, before taking the vast, deposited path angling back to the right. Go through the gate by light woods then bend sharply left past the trees to rejoin the lake at a headland overlooking Otterbield Bay. Curve back by the shore through parkland into the woods, following the lakeside path down to the jetty at High Brandelhow. Easy enough, but what a sublime route, pitching and rolling within the canopy of ancient woods, from tiny elevated headlands to the stony shores of the bays in between: easily the best of Derwentwater. Back at the landing stage, hail the launch (clockwise) for a final, waterborne look back at Brandelhow (1h30).

Brandelhow Park & the National Trust

In 1902, the 108 acres of Brandelhow Park, under threat from housing, became the first property purchased by the National Trust (for £6500, raised in less than six months). On 6 October 1902, the estate was opened at a ceremony attended by the Trust's three founders – Octavia Hill, Sir Robert Hunter and Canon Hardwicke Rawnsley (vicar of Crosthwaite, Keswick) – together with its President, Princess Louise, daughter of Queen Victoria, the four each planting an oak at the western edge of the estate. From that first acorn (as it were), the Trust today owns around a quarter of the National Park, and is easily the largest single landowner. To mark the centenary of the acquisition in 2002, a carved wooden sculpture of a giant cupped hand, entitled Entrust, was unveiled by Victoria Bay.

An alternative Catbells

▲ Maiden Moor (576m), Catbells (451m)

Distance 9.5km **Time** 3 hours 45
Height gain 670m **Map** OS Explorer OL4
Access the Keswick Launch sails hourly
across Derwentwater to High
Brandelhow. The 77/77A Honister
Rambler from Keswick passes this way
and should drop/collect from the road
north of Manesty Park (although there is
no official stop)

**Oddly overlooked, the ascent to Nitting
Haws is one of Borrowdale's best.
Combine with a crossing of Maiden Moor
and a return over Catbells for a perfect
illustration of how valley, fell and
lake connect.**

Start at the High Brandelhow landing
stage, Derwentwater (GR251197). Walk
south by the lake – around the spoilheaps,
across Brandelhow Bay and in front of the
whitewashed cottage – to a lane into the
superb Manesty Woods (NT), rising on a
gentle upward meander to the road. Walk
downhill for 150m, then turn right just
before Manesty Cottages on a narrow
rising path (SP Hollows Farm). This levels
out above the cottages to pass through a
pine copse, before weaving through
bracken to the right of a wall. Just past a
ford, an excellent view opens ahead of the
row of crags from Nitting Haws to Blea
Crag. From here, trend up to meet a more
defined path bringing you to a footbridge
back by the wall. Follow the wall to a fence
(do not cross the stile), shadowing this in
turn to a gate 100m on.

A green path now leads to a series of
small zigzags climbing sharply to the left
of a wooded ravine. With an easing of the
gradient into the combe beneath the
crags, move to the top of the grassy
shoulder to the south – Cockley How.
Press on for a further 50m to join a
pronounced rake inclining south beneath
the crags to a natural breach behind the
compact rock cone of Nitting Haws. Move
up the few paces to the top, a superb eyrie
perched above the edge of Borrowdale
(GR243168) (1h45).

Resume west by a narrow path into a
shallow, rugged and heathery
amphitheatre unseen from below, staying
to the north of the beck. Ascending the

steepening back of the bowl, look for a distinct crossing left of two tributaries, then continue west as before, out of the heather and up a slightly dull and sometimes damp grass slope, aiming for the right (north) of the rock dome on the skyline (Minum Crag). To the crest of the ridge there is now only the faintest sense of a frequented route and only occasional small cairns to mark the way ahead, but with a direct line to the north of the crag there are no difficulties.

Gaining the scarred route along the top of the ridge bear north, branching almost immediately NNE to a cairn marking the northern extent of the High Spy summit plateau (GR236171). The summit proper, only 20m higher, lies 1km SSW. Head west to rejoin the main path, which as the ridge briefly narrows drifts over to the Newlands side. As the main path peels away to the right, continue north along a thin line above crags to the most precipitous of these, Bull Crag (GR237183), marked by a humble cairn just north of the actual and barely perceptible top of Maiden Moor. Continue around to the east to rejoin the main route, descending northeast down a wide and conspicuously eroded slope back to the Borrowdale side. Drop to the col at Hause Gate and then

ascend the easy southern flank of Catbells to its bare rock summit (GR244198) (3h15).

It is an entertaining descent down the steeper northern side, with any number of variations available amongst the erosions, outcrops and minor crags. Making the level section along Skelgill Bank, split immediately right through bracken on an obvious path dropping sharply in a wide curve back to the east. Reaching the bridleway, bear right for a gentle perambulation to the road. Cross to steps; descend by a post & wire fence through more bracken to a gate. Pass through and walk beneath pines to return to the High Brandelhow landing stage (3h45).

In the Jaws

▲ King's How (392m)

Distance 3.5km Time 1 hour 30
Height gain 315m Map OS Explorer OL4
Access the 78 Borrowdale Rambler stops
by the entrance to the Bowder Stone
car park (NT)

**Find, deep in the craggy alpine heart of
the 'Jaws of Borrowdale', a short walk fit
for a King.**

Start at the Bowder Stone car park (the
former Quayfoot Quarry), off the B5289
between Grange and Rosthwaite
(GR253168). Walk through the car park to a
gate at the northern corner of the top
terrace. Join a path contouring north
through bracken for 400m to a junction
with a more frequented path rising from
the left. Turn uphill, passing over the
brow and through a gate to a wooded
hollow. Bear right at the fork and begin a
sharp ascent through the woods on a
pitched stone staircase. Gaining the
shoulder, walk ahead to a post & wire
fence, but do not cross the stile; instead,
shadow the line of the fence right, up to
the depression at Long Moss. Partially
round the knoll to the right, then break
ahead by a distinctive yew tree up a
narrow path twisting back through
heather towards the Borrowdale side.
Look out for the memorial tablet to the
then recently-deceased King Edward VII –
in whose memory the fell was donated to
the nation by his sister, Princess Louise
– just beneath the tiny, cairned summit
(GR258166). The views – north over
Derwentwater to the Skiddaw massif,

The Bowder Stone

If somewhat denuded of its mysteries by the ladder leant against its side (as it has been since Victorian times) and by the resulting polish from hundreds of thousands of feet across its top, the angled heft of the Bowder Stone remains a striking, if peculiar, sight. Most likely deposited by glacial action rather than by a tumble from the surrounding crags, it stands 10m high and 30m in circumference, with an estimated weight of 2000 tonnes. The stone has been captured in watercolour and pencil by Joseph Wright of Derby (1786, held by the Abbot Hall Art Gallery, Kendal) and more famously in oil by Atkinson Gramshaw (c.1863-68, in the collection of Tate Britain), presented as a typically awe-inducing example of its apparently wild and rough setting.

Grange

River Derwent

B5289

Greatend Crag

memorial

King's How

Long Moss

Bowder Stone

G r a n g e F e l l

Brund Fell

0   500m

west to Castle Crag and High Spy, and south down Borrowdale – are all suitably majestic.

Descend initially south, cut right on a channel between two crags and resume south to a wall. Bear right and follow this in descent by the tight zigzags of a steep and rather uneven path. Approaching a spur with a holly tree upon it, go left through an obvious break in the wall and slant south with Rosthwaite in sight, then curve directly down the slope and around to the right once on level ground. Go through the small gate to the road and turn right. After 125m, branch right on a bridleway inclining back into the woods (SP Bowder Stone). This very easy track leads past the Bowder Stone to conclude at the car park after 750m (1h30).

◀ Small hill, big views: Derwentwater and the Skiddaw massif from the top of King's How

Borrowdale condensed

▲ **High Doat** (283m), **Castle Crag** (290m)

Distance **7km** Time **2 hours 30**
Height gain **315m** Map **OS Explorer OL4**
Access **Seatoller (and Rosthwaite too) is
served by the 78 Borrowdale Rambler
from Keswick**

**From High Doat in the south to Castle
Crag in the north, from the miners' path
in the west to the River Derwent in the
east, a low-level celebration of
Borrowdale's compact variety.**

Start from the National Trust car park,
Seatoller (GR245137). Walk through the
gate at the rear of the car park, then slant
right to take the higher branch of a forking
path up to another gate. Follow the track
beyond by a wall for a short, steep pull
directly up the slope. The gradient soon
eases and a more defined green path
emerges through an increasingly rock-
decorated landscape. Pass through a gap
in a wall and then arc left with the path to

the top of High Doat: the summit is just
south of the path (GR247144).

Back at the path, continue off the top,
cross a wall to the west and descend in
this direction over a shallow depression
to a ladder stile straddling the intake wall.
Cross here to a beautifully engineered
miners' way and contour north.
Delightfully rugged, with the cuts of three
tumbling gills off Low Scawdel and an
elevated perspective over Borrowdale, this
is one of the most enjoyable routes in the
National Park.

After around 1.5km, just as the path
begins the descent into the narrow valley
west of Castle Crag, branch right on a thin
path by crags. Follow this round to level
ground and over a ladder stile. Climb to
the remains of quarry workings, where a
trenched zigzag twists between stacked
slate spoil. A clear path leads through the
pines above and the elegant circular top,
with war memorial and cairned tor, is

soon reached (GR249159) (1h20). This remarkable little fell is replete with quirks and interesting corners – if time permits, snoop around a little. Return back through the trees and the zigzag to a ladder stile around 50m above the one crossed on the way up. Over this, bear east (left), following a wall which curves right into woods. Descend through the trees to reach the side of the River Derwent and head upstream.

After 300m, cross to the other bank at New Bridge and amble up the farm track into Rosthwaite. Turn right after Yew Tree Farm (opposite the excellent Flock In tearoom) and follow the road through the village for 150m to a lane on the right, just past Larch Cottage. Turn a short way down the lane to a stile on the left, picking up a path traversing the fields behind the houses. By a whitewashed cottage, turn right along the road and over the bridge spanning the Derwent into the grounds of the youth hostel. Walk past the front of the building into riverside woods, where an entertaining (if potentially awkward) negotiation of roots and rock culminates in a step down off a boulder. The easy path beyond skirts the southern edge of the trees, rising gently behind Glaramara outdoor centre to meet the outward route (2h30).

The Professor of Adventure

Castle Crag was the summer home of a true English eccentric, Millican Dalton, the self-styled Professor of Adventure. From the 1920s to just before his death, aged 80, in 1947, Dalton lived within a pair of caves by High Hows Quarry on the eastern side of the hill, one of which bears his carved inscription 'don't waste words, jump to conclusions'. Philosophically committed to an outdoor life, he was remarkably self-sufficient, growing potatoes and baking bread on the fell. What money he needed was earned as a guide, his card promising 'Hair Breadth Escapes'. Sporting a full beard, home-made clothes and a Tyrolean hat, the teetotal, vegetarian and pacifist Dalton was regularly to be seen drifting along the Derwent upon his ramshackle raft.

Eagle's dare

▲ **Eagle Crag** (521m)

Distance 7km **Time** 2 hours 45
Height gain 440m **Map** OS Explorer OL4
Access the junction of the Borrowdale
and Stonethwaite roads is served by the
78 bus. Parking at Stonethwaite is very
limited – consider parking in Rosthwaite
and following the route to Stonethwaite
Bridge in the following walk

A stiff but exhilarating ascent is capped
by one of the very best summits in the
Lakes, an open rock shelf perched above
the confluence of the Langstrath and
Greenup valleys. A roaming descent to
Greenup Gill only adds to the fun.
Route-finding skills and a clear head
are musts.

Start at the red telephone box,
Stonethwaite (GR262137). Walk up the
road towards the valley head, opting for
the field track beyond the Langstrath Inn.
Follow this through the campsite,
drawing closer to the river as you do. After
two swing gates prefer the riverside to the
main path for a close-up of the
spectacular waterfalls and pools by
Galleny Force; stay with the curve of the
beck to rejoin the main route. Walk up
through a gate and cross the beck at a
footbridge 150m on.

Round the base of the ridge (where it
can become wet underfoot), staying right
of the fenced field to chart a way east
through bracken to the wall before
Greenup Gill. Turn upstream on a thin

Stonethwaite

Stonethwaite Beck

campsite

Galleny
Force

Alisongrass
Crag

Bleak
How

Greenup Gill

Long
Band

Heron
Crag

Eagle
Crag

Sergeant's
Crag

0   1km

path to just after a second wall descending from Bleak How. To the left of this wall, head directly up the steep bracken-thick slope (there is no path). This can be hard going – next to the wall is usually the least demanding line. As the wall approaches its top by Bleak How (the crags ahead and to the right) pick up a faint path inclining south towards a shoulder beneath the main crags to the left.

Negotiate a broken fence at a rickety stile and cross the shoulder for 50m to a gully, the only practicable breach in the crags. An easy scramble leads out to a move right on a slanting white rock platform with some exposure. Contour round to the western (Langstrath) side of the fell, then work up a succession of grass terraces stepped by rock slabs. From zigzagging along the terraces to a more direct scramble there are any number of enjoyable variations up to the neat rock summit (GR275121) (1h30).

Off the top join the path south towards Sergeant's Crag for 100m then cross the ladder stile by the corner of the wall. Bear southeast for 250m to bypass the abrupt Pounsey Crag (where a route by the descending wall will prematurely end) then strikeout east over steep springy grass and scattered rock down the broad slopes to Greenup Gill, which (unless in spate) is easy to ford. Once crossed, turn down the bridleway (which has a rather loose, rocky bed) to sweep gradually into the valley, meeting Stonethwaite Bridge after almost 3km. Cross here to return to the village (2h45).

◀ Eagle Crag

Across Rosthwaite Fell

▲ **Bessyboot** (550m),
Rosthwaite Cam (612m)

Distance 8.5km **Time** 3 hours 30
Height gain 575m **Map** OS Explorer OL4
Access Rosthwaite is served by the 78
Borrowdale Rambler from Keswick

**Is there really a lonely, undiscovered
country at the head of Borrowdale?
Explore Rosthwaite Fell's forgotten
patchwork of knolls, troughs and crags
to find out for yourself. Bring your
navigation skills and prepare for
an adventure.**

Start at the bus stop on the B5289 at the
northern edge of Rosthwaite (GR258148).
Take the lane to Hazel Bank, cross the
bridge over Stonethwaite Beck and turn
right onto an enclosed, loosely-stoned
path (SP Stonethwaite). Wind between
pastures for 1.25km on this old, largely
walled packhorse route. Bear right to cross
Stonethwaite Bridge and then left in the
village towards the valley head, taking the
stony lane beyond the Langstrath Inn.

Turn right after 500m through the gate
opposite the entrance to the campsite and
take the right-hand path, ascending into
trees by Big Stanger Gill.

Follow the beck up a steepening slope,
aiming for the depression on the horizon
between Alisongrass Crag to the south
and the distinctive cone of Hanging
Haystack to the north. The footing is
initially awkward with a jumble of roots
and rocks to weave around, but soon
enough an old pitched path emerges,
rising above the water to a stone stile.
Further ascent quickly leads to a small
depression beneath Alisongrass Crag with
the gradient easing out beyond to pretty
much level ground.

Stay with the left bank of the beck as it
turns west to a small waterfall, crossing
just before it. Resume west on an initially
faint path that soon dissolves in a soggy
bowl rounded to the south by a rough
semicircle of ridges and crags. Closer in,
north-south channels separate the spurs
off this higher ground. After the third of

◀ Above Stonethwaite: the breach between Alisongrass Crag and Hanging Haystack

these, cross back over the beck and pick a way up a prominent grassy ridge (small crags easily avoided). Follow the springy green top south for 200m, then move west up another short slope. Cross west over a hollow and gain the cairned summit of Bessyboot with a view opening over Tarn at Leaves towards the perched rock crown of Rosthwaite Cam (GR258125).

Make a short descent south on an intermittent path, passing between a low knoll and the west shore of the tarn, before rising – in the same direction – over a succession of folds to Rosthwaite Cam. No path guides this enjoyable ascent so simply pick the most interesting line, and while low crags and wet patches proliferate, none present any particular problem and are easily avoided. The Cam itself is best approached from the southeast, gaining a line north to scramble over the rough boulders to the summit (GR255118) (2h15).

Retrace the route back to the foot of the ascent from the Tarn at Leaves basin. Before the knoll to the west, turn left down a faint path, initially following the northern bank of Rottenstone Gill. As the landscape opens out, roam down the broad grass slope into The Combe, drifting slightly north to cross a beck. Go through a gate by a sheepfold and join a rough stone path that contours ENE for 700m

before dropping as a permissive path to a gate on level ground. Cross the next field to a further gate, beyond which a track leads around to a farmyard. Go through this, pass the whitewashed parish church and turn left at the road. From the crossroads with the B5289, walk ahead for 200m to a footpath branching right at a left-hand bend. Walk through fields behind a line of houses to a lane, bearing right to the road and then left through Rosthwaite to return to the start (3h30).

The face of Great End

▲ Great End (910m)

Distance 11.5km **Time** 4 hours 45 **Height gain** 835m **Maps** OS Explorer OL4 and OL6 **Access** Seatoller is served by the 78 Borrowdale Rambler from Keswick. What appears to be abundant roadside parking by Seathwaite fills quickly – late arrivals may have to consider the NT car park in Seatoller

Forget convention on this invigorating alternative to Scafell Pike. Ascend past the finest waterfall in the Lakes to the head of the celebrated Styhead Pass, then forge a dramatic line to the darkly imposing Great End. Return through a hidden bowl to join the legendary Corridor Route. Sharp navigation skills are essential.

Start at the road end, Seathwaite (GR235122). Walk through the archway opposite the farmhouse (SP Footpath & Campsite) to a walled path leading to a footbridge over Grains Gill. Cross this and turn upstream. Follow the vague route around a profusion of scattered rocks and over otherwise rather coarse and wet ground, at first by the gill, then with a marginal upward drift to a gate. Contour across the next field to a ladder stile, then trend SSW along an intermittent path up towards the wooded ravine right of the facing ridge, Seathwaite Fell.

As the high falls of Taylorgill Force come into view, stay right beneath developing crags to a gate. Now make a glorious and relatively easy scramble up the stacked boulders lining the edge of the ravine to gain a solid path arcing across scree to the pine copse at the top of the falls. (For each person along this route, at least 25 will be bound for Sty Head via Stockley Bridge: this is never a busy section, even in summer.) Press on upstream, taking in a bouldery and likely wet section prior – in quick succession – to levelling out, the joining of the main path from the far bank and the first appearance of the Scafell massif.

Skirt Styhead Tarn, continuing up to the stretcher box at the top of the pass (GR218095) (1h15). Bear east on the Esk Hause path, walking left of the crags at the

the head of the Skew Gill ravine. Walk into this and locate an obviously tried and tested route scrambling up the crags to the right. Work up the steep grass slope beyond, trending left to above a scree run. A brief traverse east here leads to a good outlook across the gullies cutting the vast north face of the mountain. A jagged but straightforward ascent south over a rock field leads to the summit plateau (GR225084) (2h45).

Cross the rough ground south to the col before Broad Crag, then bear west to the head of Greta Gill. Follow the stream – to the left is perhaps more forgiving – down into the combe beneath Broad Crag. Before the knoll of Round How ahead, branch right (NNW) into a trough beside a subsidiary beck. Within riotous mountain scenery, descend a steep grass slope to the left of the beck to meet the Corridor Route. Turn right for a gradual, rolling descent NNE along this wonderful if sometimes busy path. Beyond Skew Gill, after 750m, crest a short incline back to the Esk Hause path, turning first left to return to the stretcher box (3h45), and then right onto the path past Styhead Tarn. Either retrace the outward route or cross the footbridge to follow the Stockley Bridge path, initially beside the beck, then pitched in descent across the nose of Seathwaite Fell to the bridge itself. Cross to the track and head downstream to return to Seathwaite (4h45).

base of The Band to shadow a minor beck.

At the point where the path crosses from the right to the left of the beck, strike out SSW up the grass slope to a depression. Skirt around to the west and ascend a wide stone chute, noting a clefted crag ahead to the right. Aim for the base of this, picking up a faint and intermittent path, its movements south and SSE (by generally the rockiest line available) marked by the occasional tiny cairn.

Coming to an open shoulder by a large cairn, undulate SSE to a grassy channel at

◀ Great End, seen from Moses' Trod, Wasdale Head

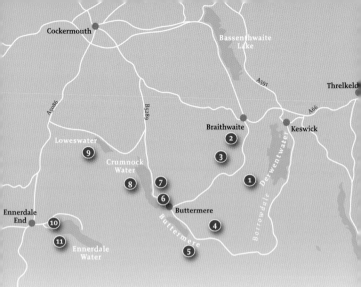

A patchwork of sleepy valleys, rolling fell ranges and small lakes, the northwest is the Lake District at its purest, and quietest. The pace of life here slips a couple of gears to leave a pleasingly remote air, as if nowhere outside mattered. No towns, no outward signs of tourism break the peace; all there is to do is to connect with the landscape. There is nowhere better.

Close to Keswick but a million miles away, the Newlands Valley is an ideal of the English landscape: a short ribbon of pea-green pastures, punctuated by spurs descending from the enclosing mountains. Pastoral and unspoiled, life consists of a couple of hamlets, a few dispersed farms, a tiny whitewashed church and a pub. Together with the fine ridges surrounding it, Newlands makes for

one of the most beautiful and rewarding places to walk in the Lake District.

A solitary through-road clings to the western rim of Newlands, bound for the least frequented pass in the National Park. Beyond it there is a more recognised and dramatic environment: Buttermere, where dark water and dark mountains collide. Convention has it to walk over Haystacks or around the lake, so do neither, and instead seek out in one direction the slender edge of Fleetwith Pike, and in the other Crummock Water, Rannerdale Knotts and that most elegant of hills, Mellbreak.

Loweswater (to the north) and Ennerdale Water (to the south) mark the last gasps of the Lake District, as the fells fade into low, round moors sliding down to the coastal plains, and the Irish Sea beyond.

Across to the High Stile ridge from Hindscarth Edge ▶

NEWLANDS, BUTTERMERE AND THE WESTERN WATERS

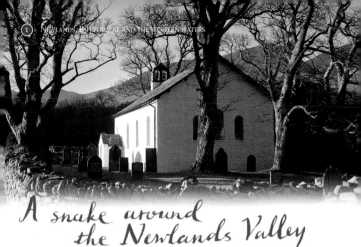

A snake around the Newlands Valley

Distance 11.5km **Time** 3 hours 15
Height gain 330m **Map** OS Explorer OL4
Access supply hardly meets demand
when it comes to parking by Hawse
End/Catbells. Spare yourself the chaos
and enjoy a bracing chug across the lake
on the launch from Keswick.
Alternatively, from March to October, the
77/77A Honister Rambler stops by the
cattle grid referred to early in the walk

Within the soft pastoral beauty of the
Newlands Valley linger the hard edges of
a long-abandoned mining industry.
Contrast the rough with the smooth on a
sinuous route through the tangled lanes,
gentle folds and lazy pastures of a
sublime valley.

Start at Hawse End landing stage,
Derwentwater (GR251213). Walk up the hill
from the lake, over the driveway to the
outdoor centre, and by the remains of a
metal fence to the road. Remain upwards,

turning right beyond the cattle grid onto
the lane to Skelgill. Just before the road
gate, step up to a wide stone path initially
rising and then contouring south above
the intake wall flanking Catbells. From
this elevated line the view opens over the
valley and the encircling ring of fells.
Approaching Yewthwaite Gill, through the
spoilheaps from one of the many former
mines, divert briefly from the wall to the
footbridge, then turn west beneath
Looking Crag towards Little Town. Do not
drop to the village; instead, leave the path
at a sharp bend above the last cottage and
walk south along a green path to meet a
much more substantial stone track
advancing towards the progressively
wilder upper reaches of the valley.

After almost 1km, as the wall to the right
withdraws, cross the footbridge over
Newlands Beck (1h). Now rise to a green
track raking right towards Low Snab Farm.
Ignore the gate into the farmyard and

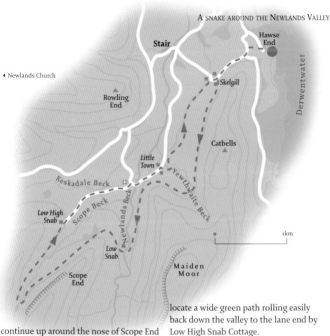

◄ Newlands Church

Stair

Hawse End

Skelgill

Rowling End

Catbells

Little Town

Keskadale Beck

Newlands Beck

Yewthwaite Beck

Derwentwater

Low High Snab

Scope Beck

Low Snab

Maiden Moor

Scope End

0   1km

continue up around the nose of Scope End into the mouth of Little Dale. At a patch of spoil, take the path branching left to a cleft cutting the fellside. Turn up a few metres to find a path traversing the western flank of Hindscarth to the small reservoir at the valley head. Hardly ever used, easy underfoot and with a strong sense of the hills, this is one of the best 'secret' paths in the Lake District.

Some 100m short of the dam, the path dissolves in a wet patch; press on to the water, a charming spot framed by Littledale Crags and waterfalls, crossing the footbridges over the outlets to the Robinson side (GR215177). Rise briefly to

locate a wide green path rolling easily back down the valley to the lane end by Low High Snab Cottage.

Descend along the peaceful metalled lane past hedgerow, pastures and scattered copses to reach the whitewashed rustic charm of tiny Newlands Church (2h30). Continue to the T-junction, turn right to cross Chapel Bridge and ascend with the road into and through Little Town. Leaving the village, take the walled lane to the right (SP Skelgill) over a ford (footbridge too) and on to its end at open fields. The way now undulates NNE across a succession of pastures to a run of three gates by Skelgill Farm. At the road, turn up to the gate across it, retracing your steps from here to Hawse End (3h15).

A Coledale trio

▲ **Barrow** (455m), **Stile End** (447m),
Outside (568m)

Distance 10km **Time** 3 hours 30
Height gain 575m **Map** OS Explorer OL4
Access Braithwaite is served by the X4/X5
bus service from Keswick and
Cockermouth. Parking is very limited,
with the most viable option a small area
400m from the village on the road to
Whinlatter (GR227237)

It is a horseshoe within a horseshoe: a
line of three neat summits tucked within
the tremendous bowl of Coledale. Follow
the airy Barrow ridge from Braithwaite to
experience a mountain landscape more
friendly than fearsome.

Start in the centre of Braithwaite at the
roadbridge over Coledale Beck (GR231235).
Walk up the lane rising from the general
store to a curving track. Follow this into
a further road, walking uphill for 150m

to a footpath on the left. Descend to a
footbridge over wooded Barrow Gill,
bearing ESE over two fields to Braithwaite
Lodge. Turn right beyond a stile (SP Public
Bridleway Newlands) to gain the foot of the
broad green path up the Barrow ridge.

Ruler-straight, the ridge offers a steady if
one-paced ascent SSW over springy grass.
There is a pleasant lofty feel, with good
views east and west, and while a couple of
false summits tease the compact top is
reached without too much effort
(GR225218). Drop west to the col at Barrow
Door, ignoring the paths breaking
southwest to Stonycroft Gill. Bear NNW up
the short slope to the head of Stile End
(GR219219) (1h30). Though little more than
a large knoll, the view west from here over
Outside to the surrounding Coledale fells
is one of the finest mountain scenes in the
Lake District. Descend WSW to the boggy
depression of Low Moss, avoiding the worst

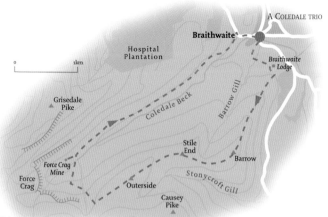

of the wet by detouring on one of the sheepruns offering a way south of the tiny hillock in its middle. From much firmer ground, rise southwest through heather on a weaving, largely trenched path dotted with corners of exposed rock to the summit of Outerside (GR209214).

Carrying on southwest, tramp down over rough grass to a strip of level ground – well to the right of the main path from Sail Pass – and on in the direction of the bowl beneath the crags at Long Comb. Reaching a small cairn around 700m off the summit, drop sharply by a faint path, moving left to cross Birkthwaite Beck. Follow a wide zigzag down to a junction

with the main Coledale Hause route, sweeping with that to a crossing of Coledale Beck at stepping stones 250m east of the Force Crag workings (2h30). With the obvious caveats about mines and old buildings, it is worth taking a closer look at these before setting off on the long stride down the track to Braithwaite.

If returning to the parking place suggested above, the track will lead you directly there, otherwise look for a path by gorse cutting down around 3km on from the beck crossing. This emerges lower down the Whinlatter road, where a simple right turn leads into the village (3h30).

Force Crag Mine

Though its pastoral tranquillity hides it well, the Newlands/Coledale area was a hubbub of mining activity for hundreds of years. Force Crag Mine, the bundle of decrepit buildings at the foot of Coledale Hause, was not only the last of these to survive but also the final metal mine to close in the Lake District. From early in the 19th century, lead was extracted here, though baryte and zinc became the emphasis in later years for a string of short-lived operations. A major collapse in 1990 flooded part of the underground workings and the mine was finally forced to close soon after. In 2004, the National Trust opened the restored processing mill for guided tours on specified dates.

Over Causey Pike

▲ **Causey Pike** (637m), **Scar Crags** (672m)

Distance 8km Time 3 hours 15
Height gain 560m Map OS Explorer OL4
Access Rigg Beck is across the Newlands
Valley from the nearest public transport
points: the cattle grid on the road above
Hawse End (served by the 77/77A
Honister Rambler from March to October)
and Hawse End jetty itself

A graceful tapering ridge soars from the
valley floor to culminate in a whimsical
summit dome, looking something like
the tip of a lemon: a simple ascent of
Causey Pike is one of the Lakes' best.

Start at the small parking area by Rigg
Beck, Newlands (GR229201). Walk north
along the road towards Braithwaite for
700m, then branch onto a thin path

breaking up the slope past the steep eastern
stub of Rowling End. Round the corner to
the Stonycroft (northern) side of the fell,
then almost immediately turn sharply left
to climb the heathery ridge. Despite – or
perhaps because of – its steepness, this is
an unfailingly entertaining ascent on a
winding, trenched path broken by slanting
rock slabs and outcrops.

Gaining the relatively level top of
Rowling End, follow the narrow path west
through heather to the cairned foot of the
summit ridge. Zigzag up the eroded,
loosely stoned slope, then make the easy
scramble (a direct assault, trending left is
perhaps best) to the head of the summit
dome (GR218208) (1h45).

Ride the waves of the ridge the short
way down to the depression before Scar

78

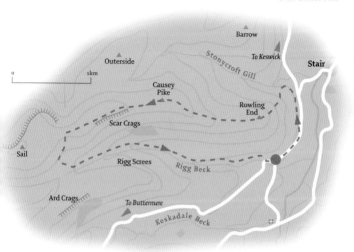

Crags, then regain height gradually, preferring the torn southern edge of the narrowing ridge for both a sense of exposure and a precipitous view to Rigg Beck. Off the top of Scar Crags (GR207206), descend WSW by a rounded, grassy slope to the col before Sail. Turn left to drop south by a narrow path hugging the eastern side of Sail; midway between col and basin look for a faint path (no more than a sheeprun) cutting directly down the slope. Join the well-graded path just above the beck, turning downstream. Cross with surprisingly firm footing the scree runs off Scar Crags, opting for the lower option at an apparent fork. The route now sweeps beside the beck – with plenty of interest but little incident – to the roadbridge by the parking area (3h15).

The Purple House

Just to the south of the roadbridge over the waters of Rigg Beck stood one of the most distinctive buildings in the Lake District: a large, North American-style wooden-clad house, painted bright purple. In its heyday from the 1950s to the 1970s, Rigg Beck (the house) had been a rare bohemian outpost in the otherwise staid Lakes. Eccentric host Varya Vergauwen ran it as an informal lodging house, entertaining poet Ted Hughes, comedienne Victoria Wood, climbers Doug Scott and Sherpa Tensing, and many actors associated with Keswick's former Century Theatre, including Tom Courtenay and Bob Hoskins. Derelict following the death of Ms Vergauwen, Rigg Beck became an increasingly sad, crumbling shadow of its former self until fire finally swept through what remained on 30 June 2008.

◀ The way over Scar Crags

Along the Edges to Buttermere

▲ Dale Head (753m), Robinson (737m)

Distance 8km Time 3 hours 30
Height gain 640m Map OS Explorer OL4
Access from March through to October
both Honister Hause and Buttermere are
linked to Keswick and Borrowdale by the
77/77A Honister Rambler. Take the 77A
bus from Buttermere to either begin or
complete the round below. The service is
infrequent, so better to begin this way

Whisper it (it won't earn you much
standing later in the bar), this is the
easiest way to any of the major ridges.
What a splendid high traverse it is too,
rolling between peaks and cols, at times
rough and narrow, at others smooth and
wide, and all within some of England's
finest mountain scenery.

Start at the road beside Honister Hause
Youth Hostel (GR225135). By a fence, walk
up the rounded grassy slope to the north.
This is a steady, if slightly dull ascent,
guided by the fence to the 600m contour,
where it peters out and from where it is a
case of pressing on NNW over an easing
gradient to Dale Head's tall, elegant
summit cairn (GR222153). This being the
head of the Newlands Valley (the 'dale'),
the view down its length is superb.

Walk west onto the immediately craggy
undulations of Hindscarth Edge, which at
its narrowest is perhaps no more than 5m
wide. There is a solid enough path, but
weaving around and over the pinnacles
along the apex is much more rewarding.
Cross the depression before Hindscarth
and then move northwest directly up the
short tail-end of the ridge, ignoring the
path branching north to the summit.
Crest for a sharp descent by the outcrops
along Littledale Edge to a second col.

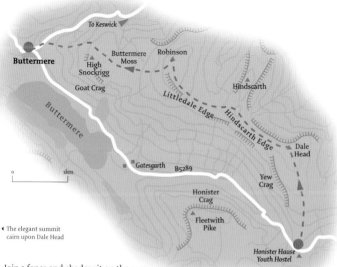

◄ The elegant summit
  cairn upon Dale Head

Join a fence and shadow it on the easy but longer climb to a large cairn on the shoulder of Robinson. Now walk north across more-or-less level ground for 300m to the smaller summit cairn (GR201168) (2h20).

Drop WSW down a steep slope to Buttermere Moss, a notorious shallow basin, where a path meanders broadly west around the worst of the marshes. Skirt to the north of the knoll of High Snockrigg, then drop by a good, partially pitched path through a series of zigzags to meet the Newlands road just above Buttermere. Turn downhill, passing the church into the village (3h30).

Bob Graham Round

In June 1932, Bob Graham, a 42-year-old Keswick guesthouse proprietor, set out from the Moot Hall to attempt a 116km (72-mile) round of 42 Lake District peaks, ascending 8000m in under 24 hours. Some 23 hours and 39 minutes later he returned and the 'Bob Graham Round', Britain's most demanding mountain run, was born. Classically, the route is taken clockwise, with the final leg the route from Honister to Robinson described here (taking in the summit of Hindscarth too), before a run out of Newlands back to Keswick. Around 100 runners (with pacesetters and support teams) take up the challenge each year, with roughly a third successfully completing within time. Billy Bland's superhuman 13 hours and 53 minutes in 1982 remains the fastest time.

From top to bottom

▲ Fleetwith Pike (648m)

Distance 5km **Time** 2 hours 45
Height gain 535m **Map** OS Explorer OL4
Access Gatesgarth is served by the
seasonal 77/77A Honister Rambler from
Keswick, Buttermere and Borrowdale

**Fire-up for an intense round through the
rocky tumult springing from the head of
the Buttermere Valley. Rise with slender-
crested Fleetwith Edge to quarried
moorland, then fall through a deep
amphitheatre beneath the ominous black
cliffs harnessing Haystacks.**

Start at the car park by Gatesgarth Farm
(GR195149). Walk up the road towards
Honister, passing Gatesgarth Cottage, to
open ground on the right. Begin to ascend
the upturned prow of Fleetwith Pike's fine
ridge, passing beneath the distinctive
white cross. A partially pitched path curves
around from the northern side back to the
middle of the ridge, where a small cairn

marks a viewpoint over the Buttermere
Valley. The route is more direct from here
– with the occasional rock outcrop
requiring use of hands – as the heathery
edge steadily narrows and steepens. In the
final 100m of ascent there is a greater
concentration of rock, though nothing
awkward, before the going eases towards
the summit cairn (GR205141) (1h15).

A good path descends gradually through
heather, bearing SSE to above the
workings at Dubs Quarry. Join a vehicle
track and follow it down by slate stacks to
Dubs Hut, then descend directly to cross
Warnscale Beck. After 30m, a thin green
path appears in the heather to the right.
Follow this as it develops into a rough
stone path descending sharply into the
superb rock amphitheatre beneath Green
Crag and the northern buttresses of
Haystacks. (A wider, smoother and less

interesting quarry path leaves Dubs Hut to the north of the beck, if you must.) From a wide 'S' bend, the rate of descent slackens and level ground is quickly reached. Cross a footbridge over the beck and walk up to the wide track sweeping out of Warnscale Bottom to the Honister road. Turn downhill to return to Gatesgarth (2h45).

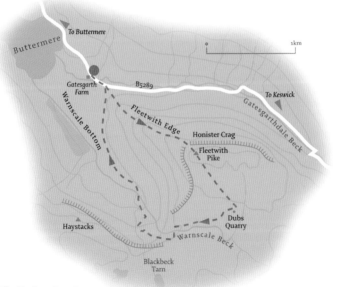

The Honister Quarries

Dubs Quarry is part of the complex slate workings reaching both within and over the surface of Fleetwith Pike. Slate has been successfully mined around Honister since the 17th century, although the recent history of the industry has been more chequered. In the 1930s, it was decided it was too costly and awkward, despite a tramway, to haul the slate from Dubs back over the moor to the centre of operations at Honister Hause. In 1986, the rest of the site closed. As a result of new ownership in 1997, the mines and inclines at the Hause were revived and today the Honister Slate Mine thrives, blending traditional mine workings with heritage tours and leisure activities – including an excellent Via Ferrata.

Buttermere's other lake

Distance **3.5km** Time **1 hour**
Height gain **100m** Map **OS Explorer OL4**
Access from **March through to October**
the **77/77A Honister Rambler** links
Borrowdale, Keswick and Buttermere

Everyone visiting Buttermere (the
village) goes to Buttermere (the lake),
but hardly anyone walks this way.
On a summer weekend that should
be all the motivation needed to enjoy a
brief introduction to the shores of
Crummock Water.

Start at the Lake District National Park
Authority (LDNPA) car park by the Fish
Hotel, Buttermere (GR173169). Walk past
the Bridge Hotel to the road, cross the
bridge and turn right onto a narrow
path heading upstream beside Mill Beck.
Weave, between lichen-covered trees, on
an elevated line above the beck to a large
and elaborate gate/step construction
straddling the wall to the left. Cross and
take the path rising ahead for a few paces
to a grassy terrace: the small knolls to the
left provide an excellent outlook. Within
200m, before the path descends, break
north over a soggy patch to locate an
intermittent path rounding a pine
coppice. On little more than a sheeprun,
contour beside a wall for 500m to beyond
a conifer plantation and then descend

gently, with opening views over Crummock Water, to a junction with a broad incline rising from the left.

Cut back down the incline to the road, then bear right for 25m to a kissing gate opening to the lake shore (SP Permissive Path). Follow the water's edge to a further stile at the end of the field, with a defined path through the wood beyond. Where this path forks, bear right to remain by the lake, crossing Mill Beck and a shingle beach to the wooded knoll of Nether How. Either follow the path around the far side of the knoll back to Mill Beck or, for greater interest, pick a way across the top to the junction. A simple stroll upstream along the southern bank of the beck, ignoring the footbridge, leads back to the start point (1h).

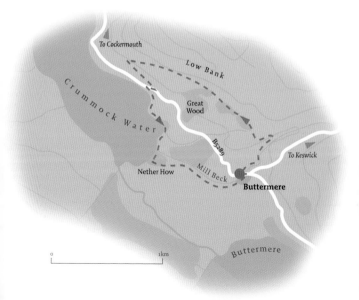

Cinderdale and Rannerdale

▲ Rannerdale Knotts (355m)

Distance 6km Time **2 hours 15**
Height gain **300m** Map **OS Explorer OL 4**
Access from March through to October
Buttermere is linked to Keswick and
Borrowdale by the 77/77A Honister
Rambler – the 77 leaves Buttermere to
pass Cinderdale Common

**Sometimes the simplest things are
best: like looping through a hidden
valley and over a stubby ridge, and all to
the side of exquisite Crummock Water.
It's wonderful at any time of year but,
thanks to the bluebells, particularly so
in late spring.**

Start at Cinderdale Common, 3km north
of Buttermere off the B5289 (GR162193).
Ascend a short way from the top of the
parking area, trending right to join a smooth
green track contouring southeast for 700m.

Continue through a gate then, 300m on,
descend to a footbridge over Squat Beck.
Separated from the beck by a wall, head
upstream into the enclosed tranquillity of
tiny Rannerdale, crossing back over the
stream 250m beyond the end of the wall as
the gradient begins to steepen.

Press on to the head of the valley (ignore
the paths shortcutting up the bank to the
right) to the open col beneath Whiteless
Breast. Turn back sharply right (WNW) onto
Low Bank, an entrancing ridge of rolls and
folds. Gradually gain height across the
undulations – keeping as far as you can
with the increasingly ragged and stony
rock crown. (A good, if less entertaining, path
leans to the Crummock side.) Although it
feels as though it ought to be, this is not
the summit of Rannerdale Knotts, which is
instead the next rise along, the

penultimate on the ridge (GR167182) (1h30).

Off the summit, drop to the next depression and then cut down to the southwest, making a sharp descent by a shattered stone staircase beside gorse. Continue steeply down over grass for a further 200m to a saddle above Hause Point, turning right (north) at the junction of paths to make the short descent to the road. Turn right again, walking through a parking area to a path sandwiched between a wall and sheer crags. Pass through a gate and tack right with the foot of the ridge back to the footbridge crossed earlier. Return over this to follow the superb path back to Cinderdale Common (2h15).

The Secret Valley

During May, the lower reaches of Rannerdale turn to a carpet of bluebells. Legend has it that these first sprang from the blood of Norman invaders, defeated in battle by native Britons concealed within Rannerdale. That, at least, was the account in The Secret Valley, Nicholas Size's historical novel of 1930. Novelist was just one of Size's accomplishments; for many years the proprietor of the Victoria Hotel (now the Bridge) in Buttermere, he had an eye for business and promoted the valley shamelessly. A parcel of land by Crummock Water was snapped up to fashion a nine-hole golf course, thus creating the Victoria Golf Hotel, while the woods opposite the hotel by Mill Beck (see the preceding walk) were purchased and marketed to tourists as 'The Fairy Glen'. Later plans, including a chairlift to the top of High Crag, mercifully went unfulfilled.

◀ Rannerdale Knotts from Cinderdale Common

A Mellbreak traverse

▲ **Mellbreak** (512m)

Distance 10km **Time** 3 hours 45
Height gain 505m **Map** OS Explorer OL 4
Access the seasonal 77 Honister Rambler
follows the B5289 between Buttermere
and Lorton. Alight at Lanthwaite Green
for a pleasant 2km walk west to the
Kirkstile Inn

Combine a traverse of the splendidly
separate Mellbreak with the shore of
Crummock Water for perhaps the best
half-day in the Northwestern Lakes. From
the stirring ascent to the unspoilt lake
shore – and not forgetting the famed
waterfall in between – it's a classic.

Start at the telephone box, Loweswater
village (GR143211). Follow the single-track
road to the Kirkstile Inn, dropping by the
negative signpost to the right-hand fork
over Church Bridge ('No through road').
Continue from the road-end at Kirkgate
Farm on to an old walled lane meandering
between lush pastures (and past a notable
earthwork, just over the wall after a sharp
left bend). Go through a gate and climb a
straight path splitting a conifer plantation
to the open fell, remaining in the same
direction to the foot of a dense scree run.
Incline left on a solid and well-worn line
across the stones, then rise by a trenched,
zigzagging path through heather,
trending gradually around to the eastern
side of the fell.

As a deep gully comes into view, make
the short scramble to the top of the first
promontory (an alternative path flanks the
gully). A line through heather and over

fractured rock leads to a second promontory, where a narrow shelf clinging to the Crummock side gives an excellent outlook over the Buttermere Valley. Remain with the nose of the fell, walking south over an eventually easing gradient to the two competing cairns of the northern summit (GR143194) (1h30).

Bear south on an easy to follow path and drop gradually to the saddle between the two summits: the character of the felltop is rather peaty with a number of potentially soggy areas to negotiate. A brief swing southeast leads into a short, steady rise up to the fanfare-free south summit (GR148186). Descend sharply south on a green path to an open shoulder by subsidiary top Scale Knott. Follow the path rounding to the west of the knoll, cross a low fence and then rake southwest down to the bridleway beside Black Beck.

Walk downstream to a footbridge over the beck, crossing to make a brief detour to view the 50m Scale Force, one of the best known waterfalls in the Lakes, 250m to the south by Scale Beck (GR151171) (2h45). Back over the bridge, continue as before, passing a wet and marshy area before branching north to the lake shore.

Weave with the lakeside path, sometimes next to the water, sometimes further away, but be sure to visit Low Ling Crag, the spit jabbing into the lake. Around 1.5km on from this, follow through bracken a gently rising path to above the field ahead. Contour through light trees to a walled lane, then turn down past a collection of cottages (Lowpark) to the road, forking left over Park Bridge. Almost immediately bear left up a charming road beside wooded Park Beck back to the Kirkstile Inn (3h45).

◀ Mellbreak towering over Loweswater (the village)

Loweswater overlook

Distance 9km **Time** 2 hours 15
Height gain 225m **Map** OS Explorer OL4
Access the seasonal 77 Honister Rambler
follows the B5289 between Buttermere
and Lorton – a kindly driver should stop
at Lanthwaite Green, where a 2.5km walk
through woods and by road leads to
Maggie's Bridge

From a lazy Sunday to a summer's
evening, any time will do for this gentle
walk on the cusp of the National Park and
the low moors of West Cumbria. Bring a
picnic and make the most of a
memorable outlook over the woods and
waters of sleepy Loweswater.

Start at the small NT parking area by
Maggie's Bridge (GR134210), between
Loweswater village and lake. Walk down
the right-hand track, heading west
towards Watergate Farm. Approaching the
farm buildings, branch onto a wide green
path directly to the gate into sylvan
Holme Wood. Now keep with the main

track beside the lake to a small stone
building. As the track veers off into the
body of the wood, stay by the shore on a
winding path that leads back eventually
to a meeting with the track at the far end
of the trees. Through the perimeter gate,
wider views of the lake open along a good
path before disappearing with the onset of
a walled lane.

By Hudson Place, take the metalled
driveway cutting across the front of the
farm for 75m to join a footpath on the left.
Follow the hedgerow to the left through
another gate, then turn sharply right
along the bottom of the field to a third
gate, beyond which the path inclines
steadily across pastures. At the next farm,
Jenkinson Place, pass above the buildings
on another metalled driveway; as this dips
to Iredale Place, split onto the stony lane
ahead. Turning uphill, the lane leads to an
open shoulder and a ladder stile over the
intake wall (1h).

Bear left along the moor-edge track for

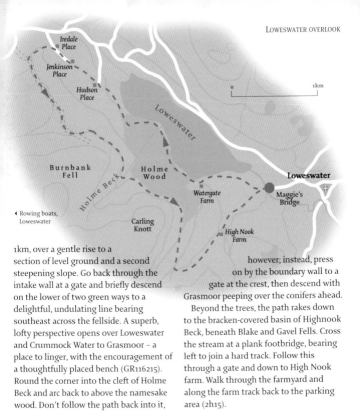

Iredale
Place

Jenkinson
Place

Hudson
Place

Loweswater

0   1km

Burnbank
Fell

Holme
Wood

Loweswater

Maggie's
Bridge

Watergate
Farm

◄ Rowing boats,
Loweswater

Holme Beck

Carling
Knott

High Nook
Farm

1km, over a gentle rise to a section of level ground and a second steepening slope. Go back through the intake wall at a gate and briefly descend on the lower of two green ways to a delightful, undulating line bearing southeast across the fellside. A superb, lofty perspective opens over Loweswater and Crummock Water to Grasmoor – a place to linger, with the encouragement of a thoughtfully placed bench (GR116215). Round the corner into the cleft of Holme Beck and arc back to above the namesake wood. Don't follow the path back into it,

however; instead, press on by the boundary wall to a gate at the crest, then descend with Grasmoor peeping over the conifers ahead.

Beyond the trees, the path rakes down to the bracken-covered basin of Highnook Beck, beneath Blake and Gavel Fells. Cross the stream at a plank footbridge, bearing left to join a hard track. Follow this through a gate and down to High Nook farm. Walk through the farmyard and along the farm track back to the parking area (2h15).

There when you need them

Break an ankle in the fells and you will soon come to appreciate the work of the Lake District's heroic Mountain Rescue teams. Every day, on average, one of them is called out to rescue the unlucky or the ill-prepared. A brief survey of the incident logs reveals that there are myriad ways in which walkers and climbers can get themselves into trouble, though injury and simply getting lost head the list. The hills around Buttermere, Loweswater and Ennerdale are served by the Cockermouth MRT, which responds to around 30-40 callouts a year. Founded in 1953, the team consists of 40 dedicated volunteer members, all thoroughly trained and with a detailed knowledge of the area. There when you need them, which hopefully will be never.

By the shores of Ennerdale

Distance 12km **Time** 3 hours
Height gain 50m **Map** OS Explorer OL4
Access Ennerdale Bridge, 2km west of the start point, is served by the rare 217 bus service from Cockermouth

Moody Ennerdale Water, the remote watery finger pointing to the celebrated mountains at the head of the namesake valley, is the only lake in the Lake District not to be bordered (at least in part) by a public road. Perfect for the walker then, and while the notorious conifers intrude upon a stretch of the northern shore, the southern shore is as good as it gets.

Start at the weir car park at the western tip of Ennerdale Water (GR085153). Walk down the path towards the lake, cross the footbridge over the outlet and follow a very easy and well-defined path down to the shore. As the path comes to the

water's edge, there are some sweeping views down the length of the lake to Pillar and the mountains beyond.

Some 1.25km on, just beyond a gate on a short stretch away from the water, be sure to turn right down the path and not proceed up the track ahead. With a feeling of a corner turned, follow the north shore along an engineered path without incident to the headland at Bowness. Here, the main path turns away from the lake to a parking area; instead, stay with a thin ribbon of path by the lake, which entertainingly dives and weaves between rocks and bracken.

Once the main path is rejoined after 800m, it has morphed into a rather dull forestry road. A speedy trudge for just over 2km leads past the end of the lake to a right turn – at the foot of the first gradient of any note – on to a parapetless vehicle

bridge over Char Dub. Follow this track to just before the wood at its head, then go through the swing gate on the right (GR130138). Keep close to the wall and pick up a path leading back through a pasture to the lake's southern shore. Once reached, the glorious character of this side of the lake is revealed: an engaging route, demanding concentration on foot placement, twists around exposed roots,

rocks and rivulets in the path bed itself. The terrain eventually relaxes somewhat. The jutting headland of Angler's Crag dominates the view ahead on this return leg and the negotiation of the path across its flank necessitates the simplest of scrambling, with a handful of rock steps and a little exposure. Back on the level, an attractive section of shoreline leads to the weir and the car park beyond (3h).

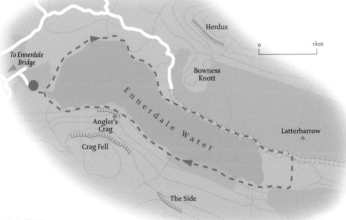

Act of Union

In her memoirs, Living History *(2003), United States Secretary of State and former First Lady Hillary Rodham Clinton discloses how, in the spring of 1973, the future 42nd President, Bill Clinton, proposed to her 'on the shores of Lake Ennerdale' (sic). The couple had been enjoying a nostalgic English tour, reliving some of Bill's haunts from his time as a Rhodes Scholar at Oxford. This pivotal moment in American political history took place at twilight, although the exact location is unknown other than to the participants. Her initial answer was 'No, not now.'*

◄ Ennerdale Water from its western tip

Ennerdale solitude

▲ Crag Fell (523m), Grike (488m)

Distance 6.5km Time 2 hours 45
Height gain 445m Map OS Explorer OL4
Access Ennerdale Bridge, 2km west of
the start point, is served by the rare 217
bus service from Cockermouth

Crag Fell and Grike are about as far
off the beaten track as it is possible to
go in the Lakes, which only accentuates
their appeal. The ascent by Angler's
Crag, the Pinnacles and Revelin Crag,
in particular, deserves a wider audience –
but in the meantime, let's keep it
to ourselves.

Start at the weir car park at the western
tip of Ennerdale Water (GR085153).
Walk down the path towards the lake,
branching right to the southern shore.
After 200m split onto a narrow path
inclining to the top of the truncated
headland abutting the water (Angler's

Crag). Detour up the few metres to the
top of the crag (GR099150), then ascend
south, soon taking a line southwest
beneath the distinctive rock fingers of
the Pinnacles. The path fades to little
more than a sheeprun, but remains
reliable, through a hollow and south
across a moorland shoulder, to gain
the western flank of the hill. Turn up
east in line with the developing edge
of Revelin Crag and by sporadic
fenceposts to the rounded summit of
Crag Fell (GR097143) (1h15).

A good path descends very gently
southwest over open moor to a saddle.
Cross the fence to the right and walk
west up an equally easy slope to the
shelter on top of Grike (GR085140) (1h45).
Strike out NNE down the springy grass of
the open fell (no path), with an excellent
view ahead of the lake. Nearing Ben Gill
and the junction with the western side of

◀ A characteristic forest, Ennerdale

Crag Fell, follow the fence east, over the stream, to where it can be easily stepped over. Join the gill downstream for 100m to the main path. Turn downhill, raking northwest into a pine wood. At an obvious fork close to the northern edge of the wood, turn directly down to a track out of the trees. Turn right and walk 125m to a stile on the left, following the track beyond to the car park (2h45).

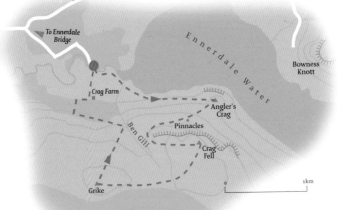

Back to nature

Ennerdale, for all its beauty, is hardly the exemplar of a natural landscape. Afforestation (and much protest) arrived with the purchase in 1925/6 of 9000 acres by the newly-formed Forestry Commission, of which 3000 acres were subsequently planted. The lake itself has supplied water to West Cumbria since 1864, with the weir added in 1902. Twice, in 1960 and again in the early '80s, plans to dam and raise the water level by around one metre were thwarted, although the initial attempt saw the demolition anyway of the waterside Angler's Inn. Today, the Wild Ennerdale project, a collaboration between local landowners the National Trust, United Utilities and the Forestry Commission, is striving for a lighter, more sympathetic approach. Blending environmental and commercial imperatives, the project aims 'to develop Ennerdale Valley as a unique wild place allowing natural forces to become more dominant in the shaping of the landscape and the ecology and, therefore, providing an inspirational visitor experience and special conservation habitats'. Amen to that.

Index